These are the best recipes of the last two thousand years.

Empires have fallen, gods have tumbled, temples have been desecrated, battles won and lost, and families divided,
but still, these recipes have survived.

Because they are our favourites.

It takes a hell of a lot to kill a good recipe. It can survive poor produce and amateur technique, thumb its nose at fashion,
and even triumph over the strange things restaurant chefs do to it,
but it won't lie down and die as long as someone still loves cooking and eating it.

To keep the good recipes good, I've cut down on fats and flours, sheared cooking times,
and used today's new freedoms and a bit of lateral thinking.

Good recipes need to evolve, change and develop with each generation's interests, skills and ingredients.

There are some things I dare not change for fear the spirits of cooks past would come and get me, but in reality,
it is change that will keep the recipes alive.

In the journey to becoming our favourite foods, many of these dishes left strange and interesting stories behind them.

I have passed them on when I have found them sufficiently amusing, but I am no historian.

Most of my sources are secondary at best, so where there is no story, I have confined myself to saying something useful.

The beginning of a new century is a good time to spring-clean our recipes, our tools and our kitchen ways;
a time to sort out what is worth taking with us into the future, and what can well be left behind.

Let us work out what we value, and dispense with the rest of the baggage.

We want food that tastes of itself, or better.

Food that makes us feel spoilt and loved.

Food that is good for us; that has generosity and personality; that doesn't damage the world around us.

Food that looks like food, not a branch of architecture, artistic fantasy, engineering triumph or animal trophy.

Food that makes great leftovers you want to eat the next morning.

We also want, and need, logical food, that behaves the way it should behave.

Natural food that is honest not phony; individual food that is rich in meaning.

Food that is cooked by one's nose, eyes and fingers, not by one's cook book, supermarket, or equipment.

Food that links us to the generations past; that has a sense of time and place; that has a reason to be;
that gives us a sense of the continuity of life;
that reminds us these things have been done before and will be done again.

Old food. Favourite food.

Above all, food that makes people fall in love with us.

That's what cooking is all about, as it always has been.

Jill Dupleix

Old Food by Jill Dupleix

New ways with old favourites

Photography by Petrina Tinslay and Ashley Mackevicius.
Design by Visnja Brdar. A Sue Hines Book.
Allen & Unwin

Pod peas.

Put flowers back on your table.

Set a proper breakfast table once a week, with home-made marmalade, real bread, and a big pot of tea.

Lick your fingers.

Think of the hen that laid your egg.

Spring clean your pantry once a year, and freshen up on spices and sauces.

Aprons are not demeaning. They are there to keep your clothes clean.

Use this book as if it were your grandmother.

Think of cooking as an escape, a nourishing ritual, a delight, something that can improve your life.

The kitchen is your playground, a sanctuary, a place of creativity and imagination.

Cooking is the sport of the future.

The ideal kitchen has room for cookbooks, music, paintings, and a computer. It is not always clean, tidy and spotless.

Good pots and pans aren't luxuries. They make cooking so much easier, they are necessities.

Cook your favourite food for your favourite people.

Life is not a smorgasbord. It's à la carte. You have to choose what to put in your body.

Eat well.

Your home is not a restaurant. Don't compete with professional kitchens, million dollar equipment and fourteen apprentices.

We can make the one thing they can't – good home cooking.

Take one step back. Buy chicken on the bone, not just fillets. Cook a whole fish.

Use brown sugar rather than white. Buy tea in leaves and coffee in beans.

The fewer machines you use, the better the food. Use the power in your hands.

Don't be scared of tripe, brains, liver and kidneys. Why eat only the outside?

Get up early and go to the market. If you're lucky enough to have a fresh food market, use it, or lose it.

The world does not need vegetable medleys. Serve one vegetable with your meal – be it meat, fish, grain or vegetable itself – and make it great.

Know where your food has been, before you work out where it is going. Buy organic and buy fresh, daily if possible.

Make friends of your shop-keepers. Buy them a Christmas present. Tell them what you are going to cook.

Give them feedback. And give them a hard time, if you have to.

Always taste, before you add salt. And always use flakes of pure sea salt.

The perfect vinaigrette is three parts oil to one part vinegar. The perfect martini is ten parts gin to one part dry vermouth.

This is probably all you need to know in life.

Cook when you're happy, not when you're angry, tired or ill.

A little butter is a wonderful thing.

Preserve your heritage. Get the three best recipes out of your grandmother now.

Something will always go wrong when you cook. It's not your fault.

Keep going.

Just don't kill anyone.

Good food is beyond fashion. It will be here forever.

Think twice before you chop everything up into little bits. Some things are beautiful when served whole.

Parsley is a herb, not a garnish.

Tuck the corner of a kitchen cloth into your belt every time you cook, and you'll always be able to find it when you need it.

The next time you are fed up with the phone, the fax, the little old men wearing hats who drive slowly in front of you,

the wars, the droughts, the fake foods and the little gooey things that go down the sink plughole, go bake a cake.

Good food does not require a frizz of deep-fried leek to sell itself.

Hot food should be served hot and cold food should be served cold.

Simple is hard. But not that hard.

Cooking takes what is bad in food and makes it good, and what is good and makes it better. Learning to cook is the process of knowing the good from the bad.

Food that survives the ages is food that is good for us.

There are ghosts in our kitchens. You can feel them as you push the onions around in a little oil, when you crush the garlic, or when you pull a cake from the oven and feel the heat against your face.

Cook with a sense of tradition, and the wisdom of past cooks will guide your hand.

Save your string. Re-use your plastic bags. Take a basket to the shops.

Let your children watch you cook.

Do not serve anything that involves celery and cream cheese.

Never slave over a hot stove.

Do the dishes as you go.

Your mother was right.

The entire medical industry was right.

The ancient peoples who broke their fast with anything from bread dipped in wine, to mutton and salt fish, or a cup of sweet coffee were right.

Even that stupid monkey on the packet of Coco Pops was right.

Breakfast is important. With breakfast inside you, you can take whatever the day will bring.

Breakfast makes you strong. If you get it right, the rest of the day will be perfect.

Therefore, we should all learn how to boil an egg properly.

We should give breakfast enough time to be of benefit to our bodies.

We should eat our breakfast sitting down at the table.

We should change our breakfast ritual with the seasons, so that a summer breakfast (fresh fruit and yoghurt) is radically different to a winter breakfast (six grain porridge).

As for popular breakfast cereals, avoid anything with added vitamins.

They are only putting back a little of what they have taken out in the puffing, popping or processing.

And don't feel you have to have a 'proper' breakfast, whatever that means.

Have an improper one, any time you like.

Serve up sweet cous cous, grilled strawberries on toast, steaming hot chocolate, frothy drinks of banana and yoghurt, and sympathetic hangover cures like grilled ham and cheese on toast.

If you don't have time for breakfast, I suggest you get to bed earlier so that you can get up earlier.

Besides, if you eat breakfast, you won't get hungry until lunch time.

You won't get that spacy, vacant feeling at mid-morning.

You won't need snacks and millions of cups of coffee.

You won't put on weight, because your weight will stabilise.

You will feel happier, healthier, and more in control.

All this, breakfast can do for you, and more.

Breakfast

Porridge plus
Strawberries on toast
Baked beans and bacon
Sweet cous cous with apricots
Feta cheese brik
Pikelets with yoghurt and honey
Banana muffins
Nasi goreng
Miso and tofu soup
Ricotta with stewed fruits
Beid hamine
Croque-monsieur

Porridge plus

Scotland's most famous food, porridge is traditionally stirred clockwise, never anticlockwise, with a straight wooden stick rather than a spoon. Yes, well. This power-packed mix of five different grains and seeds from your nearest health food store will give you so much energy, you'll probably whizz them as fast as a food processor. Just think risotto: calm down and stir slowly and steadily.

1kg (2 lb) rolled oats
250 g (9 oz) barley flakes
250 g (9 oz) rye flakes
100 g (3½ oz) sesame seeds
50 g (1¾ oz) linseed

Mix all grains, and store in an airtight jar.

Mix 2 cups of grains with 2 cups of cold water in a saucepan, stirring briskly with a wooden spoon until creamy. Add 3 cups cold water and bring to the boil, stirring. Reduce heat to a simmer, and cook for around 10 minutes, stirring occasionally until grains are soft and bouncy, and the pot suddenly smells sweet and porridgey.

Pour into bowls, and serve. Top with a sprinkling of brown sugar or honey, and a little milk.

Feeds four, several times over.

Strawberries on toast

I'd love to call this strawberry bruschetta, but I'm not that cute. The French and Italians have been serving fruit on toasted bread or brioche for many years, before the rest of us caught up with the idea. Here, fresh, sweet strawberries melt under a sugary glaze on grilled country bread. In summer, try it with fresh plums, sliced peaches, or your favourite berries. And call it bruschetta.

4 thick slices country bread, day old
2 punnets strawberries, washed then hulled
2 tbsp caster sugar
4 tbsp mascarpone cream
icing sugar

Grill bread on one side only. Slice strawberries thickly, and pile onto ungrilled sides, covering right to the edges.

Sprinkle caster sugar on top, and place under griller for 2 minutes until sugar caramelises into a golden glaze, watching that bread does not burn.

Dollop mascarpone cream on top. Dust with icing sugar, and serve hot.

Feeds four.

Baked beans and bacon

Do not wake up in the morning and spontaneously decide to have this for breakfast. Instead, wake up yesterday morning and decide to have it for breakfast today. (Okay, okay, or wake up today and have it tomorrow). Home-made baked beans are a billion times better than the canned variety, but with the same alchemy of sweet and smoky flavours.

500 g (1 lb) white beans
1 onion
2 cloves
4 thick slices of smoky bacon, speck or kaiserfleisch
1 onion, finely chopped
400 g (14 oz) canned tomatoes, mashed
1 tbsp brown sugar
4 tbsp maple syrup
2 tbsp Worcestershire sauce
1 bay leaf
1 tsp sea salt
½ tsp freshly ground black pepper
1 extra tbsp brown sugar

Cover beans with cold water and soak for 6 to 8 hours.

Drain and place beans in a large pot. Cover with cold water, add the onion spiked with the cloves, and bring to the boil. Simmer for 1½ hours or until tender. Drain the beans, and discard onion and water.

Heat oven to 160°C (325°F). Cut rind from bacon and cut into cubes. Cook bacon and chopped onion in the base of a lidded, ovenproof casserole, until the bacon crisps slightly and the onion is soft. Add tomatoes, brown sugar, maple syrup, Worcestershire sauce, bay leaf, sea salt and pepper and mix well. Add the drained beans and 2 cups of cold water, stir, then cover tightly.

Bake in the oven for 2 hours, then give it a big stir, adding a little water if it seems dry. Sprinkle with extra brown sugar, and bake uncovered for another 20 minutes, until glazed on top. Serve with, or on, thick slices of grilled bread.

Feeds six.

Sweet cous cous with apricots

Have a bowl of one of the oldest cereals in the world: dusky, cinnamon-spiced cous cous, served with warm, spiced milk and sweet apricots in syrup – or fresh ripe figs in season. This recipe uses packaged cous cous, and feeds eight to ten, so ask your friends around and serve it for brunch, or you'll be living on it for a week.

500 g (1 lb) dried apricots
3 tbsp sugar
500 g (1 lb) cous cous
500 ml (18 fl oz) boiling water
2 tbsp extra virgin olive oil
50 g (1¾ oz) unsalted butter, cut into small dice
1 tbsp ground cinnamon
50 g (1¾ oz) sugar
1 litre (1¾ pints) milk
1 vanilla bean, split
1 cinnamon stick
1 tsp clear rose water syrup

Soak apricots in water to cover, overnight.

Drain water into a saucepan, add sugar and bring to the boil, stirring. Return apricots to syrup, cook for 10 minutes or until soft and luscious, and leave to cool.

Place cous cous grains in a big, wide bowl. Pour boiling water evenly over the top, then drizzle with extra virgin olive oil, cover bowl and leave to rest for 5 minutes. Work the butter through the cous cous with your hands, coating the grains well, until cous cous feels light and fluffy. Mix cinnamon and sugar and rub through cous cous just before serving.

Heat milk, vanilla bean and cinnamon stick to just below the boil. Remove from heat, add rose water, and strain into a jug. Place cous cous in cereal bowls, dusted with a little extra ground cinnamon.

Serve with a bowl of apricots and their syrup, and the jug of warm spiced milk.

Feeds eight to ten.

Feta cheese brik

Something like a large, flat, failure of a spring roll, a brik is a Tunisian pastry, traditionally made from skin-thin sheets of warkha pastry which take centuries to learn how to make. A packet of Asian spring roll wrappers from an Asian food store freezer, on the other hand, takes only minutes to learn how to open. Hopefully.

4 large spring roll wrappers
1 cup feta cheese
2 tbsp finely chopped parsley
2 tbsp finely chopped coriander
vegetable or light olive oil for frying
1 tsp cornflour mixed with 1 tbsp cold water
1 tsp sea salt
½ tsp freshly ground black pepper
1 tsp ground coriander
½ tsp ground cumin
4 free range eggs

Remove wrappers from freezer 10 minutes prior to cooking. Mash feta cheese with parsley and coriander. Heat oil in a wok or frypan to 2.5 cm (1 in) deep. Mix salt, pepper, coriander and cumin in a small bowl.

Place one spring roll wrapper on workbench. Dip finger in cornflour mixture and run along edges. Lay sheet over a bread and butter plate, to form a slight hollow in the centre. Spread a tablespoon of the herbed cheese in the centre. Crack one egg, discard white, and gently place the yolk in the centre of the cheese. Sprinkle with a little of the spice mix. Draw the edge of pastry closest to you over the egg, about two-thirds towards other end, working quickly. Fold the far end of pastry towards you, and pinch the ends tight to seal them.'

Slip package from the plate into the hot oil, and cook for around 3 minutes turning once – by then the pastry should be golden and the egg inside still slightly soft. Drain on paper towel. Cook remaining parcels and serve immediately.

Feeds four.

Pikelets with yoghurt and honey

Pikelets are also called drop scones, because of the way you drop the batter into the frypan. They're cute and fresh and rather housewifely, even when topped with thick yoghurt and drizzled with honey. If the housewifely reference gives you the horrors, top them with caviar instead and to hell with the housework.

140 g (5 oz) self-raising flour
pinch of salt
2 tbsp sugar
2 eggs, beaten
180 ml (6 fl oz) milk
1 tsp melted butter
extra butter for the pan
500 ml (18 fl oz) natural yoghurt
1 cup fresh walnuts
your favourite honey, gently warmed

Sift flour and salt into a large bowl. Add sugar. Beat in eggs and then milk until mixture is smooth. Stir in melted butter.

Heat a non-stick pan with a little butter until surface is covered. Drop spoonfuls of batter into the pan, three or four at a time. Cook for a couple of minutes until bubbles appear on the surface and base is golden. Flip them over, and cook other side until lightly golden.

Stack pikelets with yoghurt and walnuts and drizzle honey on top, or serve them still warm, with bowls of yoghurt, honey and walnuts on the side.

Makes twelve to sixteen.

Banana muffins

Buttermilk – originally the milk left after cream is churned into butter – gives these muffins a nicely sour tang, balanced by sweet bananas. Like all muffins, these are better warm from the oven than cold. They team very nicely with baked rhubarb (Pantry, 216).

200 g (7 oz) plain white flour
2 tsp baking powder
pinch of salt
80 g (3 oz) bran
½ tsp ground cinnamon
¼ tsp ground cloves
¼ tsp ground nutmeg
2 eggs
150 g (5¼ oz) raw sugar
3 tbsp vegetable oil
250 ml (9 fl oz) buttermilk or milk
1 ripe banana, diced

Sift flour, baking powder and salt together in a bowl. Add bran and spices, and mix well. Beat eggs, sugar, oil and buttermilk together, in a second bowl. Add banana and stir. Make a well in the centre of the dry ingredients, and add the egg mixture, stirring roughly with a fork, without over-mixing.

Pour or spoon batter into lightly buttered muffin tray cups or individual muffin cases, until three-quarters full. Bake at 200°C (400°F) for 20 to 25 minutes, or until muffins come away from the side of the pan when touched.

Serve on their own or with a fruit compote.

Makes ten.

Nasi goreng

Beautiful Bali's favourite breakfast for locals and tourists alike, nasi goreng is just a simple fried rice studded with freshly made omelette strips, bean shoots and vegetables. Toss in leftover cooked chicken or ham if you like, or top with a fried egg and a hit of chilli instead of the delicate omelette thingy.

3 tbsp peanut oil
2 eggs, well beaten
1 small onion, finely chopped
1 carrot, finely diced
1 cup bean shoots, washed
1 tsp chilli sambal (sambal oelek), to taste
1 tbsp tomato sauce
2 tbsp soy sauce
2 cups shredded iceberg lettuce
3 cups cooked jasmine rice, chilled
2 tbsp deep-fried shallots
8 sprigs coriander

Heat wok or frypan until hot. Add one tablespoon of the oil, and swirl the pan around so that a thin film of oil covers the sides. Add beaten eggs and swirl again so that a thin film of egg covers most of the surface. Cook quickly until egg sets, then loosen it with a knife and tip it out onto a large plate. Roll omelette into a cylinder and cut into thin slices.

Heat remaining oil in wok or frypan, and fry onion and carrot until soft, tossing well. Add bean shoots, chilli sambal, tomato sauce, soy sauce and half the shredded lettuce and toss until well mixed, and the vegetables are tender.

Scatter rice on top of mixture with your hands, breaking up the clumps. Toss well over until rice is hot, and well coloured by the sauces. Adjust flavour by adding more of the sauces if desired. Add omelette strips, remaining lettuce and fried shallots, toss through and divide among serving bowls or plates. Scatter coriander on top and serve.

Feeds four.

Miso and tofu soup

It's delicious! It's nutritious! It probably even has riboflavin in it! Miso soup is one of the oldest soups in the Japanese repertoire, and one of the handiest at breakfast time or any time. Just add a few squares of fresh bean curd (tofu) and a little chopped green (spring) onion for a beautiful breakfast that didn't come from a box of cereal.

1 litre (1¾ pints) dashi broth (Broths and Sauces, 206)
2 tbsp mirin
2 tbsp light soy sauce
3 tbsp red miso paste
3 beancurd squares

Heat dashi broth to just below the boil and add mirin and soy sauce, stirring. Remove three tablespoons of broth and cool to lukewarm. Place miso paste in a bowl and whisk into a paste with the three tablespoons of dashi broth. Pour the miso paste very gradually back into the simmering broth, stirring constantly until dissolved.

Cut beancurd into small cubes and add to the gently simmering broth. Add any vegetables in small pieces, and heat through *without boiling*. (That's printed in italic so that you remember *not to boil it.*)

P.S. Look for red miso paste, a fermented and aged soybean paste, at health food stores and Japanese groceries.

Feeds four.

Ricotta with stewed fruits

Buy your ricotta from a large, fresh round, rather than in a supermarket packet, and you'll fall in love with its sweet, innocent freshness. Serve it in its natural state as you see it here if you're feeling non-interventionist, but it is especially delicious when eaten warm from the oven where it softens into a sort of heavenly, delicate dessert that tastes as if it took eighteen apprentices to make it.

500 g (1 lb) dried figs, peaches, pears, apples
1 bay leaf
1 cup brown sugar
1 cup dry white wine
2 cinnamon sticks
1 vanilla bean, split
750 g (1½ lb) wedge of fresh ricotta, drained
1 tbsp white sugar

Soak dried fruits and bay leaf overnight, in enough cold water to cover.

Transfer fruits and their soaking water to a saucepan, and add sugar, wine, cinnamon and vanilla bean, adding a little more water to cover if necessary. Cook gently for 30 minutes, stirring occasionally, until fruit is soft and liquid is syrupy.

Heat oven to 180°C (350°F). Place ricotta in baking pan, cover with foil, and bake for 30 minutes. Remove foil, sprinkle with white sugar, and bake for another 10 minutes until lightly golden on top (use an overhead grill for faster results, but keep an eye on it).

Serve a scoop of warm ricotta into each bowl and top with warm stewed fruits and a good spoonful of syrup.

Feeds four.

Beid hamine

You can forget your three-minute boiled egg. This ancient Moroccan technique is one of the slowest ways to cook eggs in the world, and yet one of the nicest, sweetest and easiest. Simmered for hours with brown onion skins, the eggs end up with a dusky brown colour, an indefinable fragrance, and a sweet, soft and creamy body. Team with grilled Turkish bread and spiced cumin salt.

8 eggs
skins from 6 brown onions
1 tbsp ground coffee
2 tsp sea salt flakes
1 tsp ground coriander
1 tsp ground cumin
1/2 tsp sweet paprika

Place eggs, onion skins and ground coffee in a large heavy-bottomed pan and fill with water. Bring to the boil, cover, and reduce heat to the lowest heat possible, preferably on a simmer pad. Simmer gently for at least 6 hours, preferably 8, topping up the water if necessary.

Remove eggs and cool to room temperature.

Mix sea salt, coriander, cumin and paprika to taste. Serve the eggs with lightly grilled Turkish bread and a bowl of the spice mix, for dipping.

Feeds eight.

Croque-monsieur

Literally translated as a gentleman's crunch, the *croque-monsieur* is a true bite of Paris, guaranteed to restore you on a-morning-after-the-night-before, even if you didn't have a night before that left you in need of restoration.

6 tbsp grated Gruyère cheese
3 tbsp sour cream
freshly ground black pepper
1/2 tsp grated nutmeg
1 tsp Worcestershire sauce
1 tsp Dijon mustard
4 thin slices good ham
8 slices fresh white bread
butter, softened

Mix grated cheese with enough sour cream to make it hold together. Add pepper, grated nutmeg, Worcestershire sauce, and mustard.

Place a sheet of greaseproof paper on the bench, butter 8 slices of bread, then turn 4 of them butter-side down. Cover the 4 unbuttered sides with the grated cheese spread, right to the edges. Top bread with slices of ham, cut to fit. Top with remaining slices of bread, butter-side up.

Heat a heavy-bottomed frypan and place sandwiches butter-side down, pressing down lightly to help them stick together. Fry until golden, then turn and fry until lightly golden on the second side. Serve hot, or have the overhead grill heated for this next optional step.

Remove sandwiches from pan and quickly spread one side with any remaining cheese mixture, covering right to the edges to prevent burning. Place under grill for one minute or two until the cheese topping bubbles and browns, watching carefully that it doesn't burn.

Feeds four.

Lunch

Never eat lunch at the desk.

Never, ever eat it driving the car.

Never, ever, ever eat it while talking on the telephone.

Lunch should be taken with a sense of achievement from the morning, and anticipation for the rest of the day.

It doesn't make sense to deny yourself lunch.

Without it, there is no progress, no vision, and no poetry.

Those who continue to work through lunch will be the slaves of the twenty-first century.

But a lunch during the week is different from lunch at the weekend.

Office lunches should be fresh and interesting, different every day.

They need to be planned and prepared, as for any important meeting.

A work-day lunch can be as simple as a ripe avocado crushed on toast, drenched in lemon juice and black pepper.

On the weekend, you might like to go to a bit more trouble, like putting it on a plate.

Weekend lunches have a sense of holiday freshness and taking it easy.

They should just happen. If they get too planned, they'll start getting as difficult as dinner.

A weekend lunch can be a slice of prosciutto on grilled bread, a poached egg on wilted spinach, or roasted mushrooms drizzled with garlicky olive oil.

When in doubt, grill a fish.

And always remember that your favourite breakfast makes a great lunch.

Scrambled eggs on toast. Sausages and baked beans.

(Raid the breakfast chapter for lunch, and the lunch chapter for dinner. You'll be out of sync with the rest of the world, but who cares?)

A freshly made sandwich makes the perfect lunch, even when entertaining.

Every lunch should come with time to enjoy it, and time to digest it.

At its most ideal, the final course is a short nap, in order to get your strength up for dinner.

Lunch

Grilled fish with olives
Hogazas
Thai beef salad
Seared tuna with egg and anchovy
Esqueixada
Fish fingers
Pork and spinach terrine
Spanakopita
Pad Thai
Pan con tomate
Rabbit rillettes
Grilled seafood salad

Grilled fish with olives

A fine mix of the fresh and the ancient on the same plate. The simplest of fish, such as little red mullet (barbounia or rouget), sardines, small mackerel or baby silver bream, are licked with balsamic vinegar and served with soft, fruity black olives and olive oil. It's like eating under an olive grove overlooking the Mediterranean.

4 small, fresh fish
2 tbsp extra virgin olive oil
1 tbsp balsamic vinegar
sea salt and freshly ground black pepper
1 cup mild and fruity black olives
2 tbsp chopped flat-leaf parsley
more olive oil and balsamic for drizzling

Scale, gut and clean fish if necessary. Heat the grill.

Mix olive oil, balsamic vinegar, salt and pepper, and brush each fish lightly with the dressing. Grill on the first side until well-marked, then carefully turn fish and grill lightly on the other side.

Cut olive meat away from the pips, and mash lightly with the back of a fork, or finely chop. Mix olive meat with parsley. Place each fish in centre of serving plate, surround with olives and parsley, and drizzle with olive oil and balsamic vinegar.

Feeds four.

Hogazas

The Spanish have a way of eating and drinking that cuts right to the soul. While tapas is traditionally an evening event, the principle of eating small snacks accompanied by a cold beer, a freshly opened, well chilled bottle of Jerez (sherry) or a glass of wine is too good not to do in the middle of the day. Hogazas (ho-garth-us) is also the name of the round Castilian bread that is most likely to be used for these tapas toasts.

round country-style loaf of bread, or a long crusty baguette
Serrano-style ham or prosciutto
vine-ripened tomatoes
wood-roasted piquillo peppers, drained
sheep's milk cheese e.g. manchego
chorizo sausages, grilled
red pepper (capsicum), roasted (Pantry, 221)
esqueixada salt cod salad (Lunch, 26)
black olives
morcilla sausages, grilled
smoked salmon, sliced
lemon
white asparagus, drained
Spanish anchovies, drained

Cut bread into long slices (if a baguette, cut on the diagonal) Grill briefly on both sides, then use any or all of the following:

top with fine slices of Spanish Serrano-style jamon (ham) or prosciutto and a slice of vine-ripened tomato, or:

top with Spanish piquillo peppers and sheep's milk cheese, or:

top with grilled chorizo sausage and roasted red peppers, or:

top with esqueixada salt cod salad and black olives, or:

top with cubes of grilled morcilla sausage, or:

top with smoked salmon and a squeeze of lemon juice, or:

top with big, fat, white Spanish asparagus and jamon, or:

top with anchovies and wood-roasted piquillo peppers.

Feeds four.

Thai beef salad

My mouth waters every time I think of this dish, with its crazy blend of hot chillies, sour lime juice, and fresh mint and coriander. Use the best beef you can find, and even the most unadventurous meat eater will be blown away. Serve with a platter of fresh raw vegetables in the centuries-old balance that makes Thai food so healthy and so lovable.

1 tbsp jasmine rice
2 dried red chillies (or ½ tsp chilli powder)
500 g (1 lb) thick fillet steak
1 tsp sugar
3 tbsp lime juice
3 tbsp Thai fish sauce
4 red shallots, finely sliced
3 tbsp mint leaves
3 tbsp coriander leaves
3 green (spring) onions, finely sliced

Heat a dry frypan, add rice and toast over medium heat until golden but not burnt. Grind rice in a clean coffee-grinder or pound to a powder and set aside.

Reheat frypan and add dried red chillies. Toast until they are smoky, then grind or pound to a powder, and set aside.

Grill or pan-fry the beef until well-marked outside, and rare to medium rare inside. Place in a bowl and leave to rest for 10 minutes.

Dissolve sugar in lime juice and fish sauce. Mix ½ teaspoon of the ground roasted chilli powder (store the rest) with ground rice. Combine shallots, mint, coriander and green onions in a large bowl. Add lime juice, fish sauce and sugar. Taste and adjust flavourings, until the salad is hot, sour, sweet and salty.

Slice the beef thinly. Toss beef and ground rice through the salad, with any cooking juices that have collected in the bowl. Pile high on a large platter and serve with a big salad of crunchy raw lettuces and cucumber, and a bowl of steamed jasmine rice.

Feeds four as part of a Thai meal.

Seared tuna with egg and anchovy

Based on the ancient Niçoise *pissala*, a paste of ground anchovies, this dish goes beyond the Niçoise salad, using green beans, fried tomatoes and a coddled egg. The two-minute egg that actually takes thirty minutes is a great little trick in its own right to use for all sorts of salads.

4 free range eggs (65 g)
6 anchovy fillets, rinsed and dried
2 tbsp red wine vinegar
freshly ground black pepper
4 tbsp extra virgin olive oil
20 green beans, trimmed
2 large round oxheart tomatoes
4 tuna steaks, cut around 2 cm (1 in) thick

Place eggs in a pan of simmering water and boil for 3 minutes. Remove from water and allow to cool for 30 minutes.

Pound 4 of the anchovy fillets to a paste. Add vinegar and pepper, and whisk in the olive oil until dressing thickens.

Cook green beans in simmering, salted water for 3 minutes. Drain, cool under cold running water and set aside. Slice each tomato into 2 large discs, discarding top and bottom discs. Fry tomatoes in a little extra olive oil on both sides until browned and soft.

Grill tuna, or sear in a hot pan for 2 or 3 minutes, then turn and quickly cook other side, leaving the centre pink. Leave to rest for 3 minutes.

Place a fried tomato in centre of each plate. Toss beans in the dressing and pile high on tomatoes. Rinse and dry remaining anchovy fillets, and cut in half lengthwise. Place tuna on top of beans, garnish with the anchovy fillet, and then drizzle with remaining dressing. Cut off the top of each egg and nestle egg to one side.

Feeds four.

Esqueixada

An unusual but very refreshing little Catalan salad (pronounced eskasharda) of salt cod topped with tomato, onion, olives and olive oil, that deserves to be served with a great Spanish sherry. Serve as an entrée or tapa, and pile high on grilled bread.

350 g (12 oz) salt cod fillet
1 small onion, finely chopped
1 ripe tomato, finely diced
1 red pepper (capsicum), cut into thin strips
10 small black olives
4 tbsp fruity olive oil
2 tbsp red wine vinegar
sea salt and freshly ground black pepper

Soak the salt cod in a big pot of cold water for 36 hours, changing the water 4 times during that time to freshen it. Soak onion in a little salted water for an hour or two.

Drain salt cod and onion, and gently squeeze dry. Separate flesh from bones and skin. Tear off thin strips of cod with your fingers (the traditional method), or carve paper-thin slices with a knife.

Layer the strips in an earthenware serving bowl, and top with onion, tomato, red pepper and olives. Mix olive oil, vinegar, salt and pepper in a small bowl and pour over the top. Cover and chill for 2 hours.

Feeds four.

Fish fingers

I know, I know, you didn't think fish had fingers, et cetera. Well, they certainly didn't have luxurious fingers of fresh, melting, buttery salmon coated in golden crumbs and served with creamy mash and a lemon-scented caper mayonnaise. My apologies to Bird's Eye, who invented the fish finger in 1946, for improving on their idea so dramatically.

4 fillets of salmon, from the thickest part
3 eggs
1 cup plain flour
salt and freshly ground black pepper
1 cup fine breadcrumbs
finely grated rind of 1 lemon
1 tbsp butter
1 tbsp light olive oil
extra lemon to serve
skin of preserved lemon, rinsed
1 tbsp capers, rinsed
1 tbsp lemon juice
6 tbsp home-made or good quality mayonnaise

Peel the skin from the fillets. Tweezer out any of the long fine bones inside. Cut two oblongs of fish from each fillet, about 3.5 cm long by 2.5 cm wide by 2.5 cm deep (3 in by 1 in by 1 in) – you can use the trimmings for a salmon omelette tomorrow.

Crack eggs into a bowl and beat lightly. Place flour, salt and pepper in a second bowl. Mix breadcrumbs and lemon rind in a third bowl.

Heat butter and oil in a frypan until hot. Dip each salmon finger into flour, then into egg, then into breadcrumbs, and place in oil. Cook gently, turning once, until lightly golden, no more than 3 or 4 minutes in all, until salmon is cooked, but still pink and moist inside. Drain on paper towel, and serve on a bed of mash with lemon wedges, and a rocket salad.

Cut preserved lemon into tiny dice. Whisk preserved lemon, capers and lemon juice into mayonnaise, taste for salt and pepper, and serve in a separate bowl.

Feeds four.

Pork and spinach terrine

There are no tricks and no surprises to a terrine. It is a faithful kitchen friend to whom we should return time and again. Slice thinly and serve with a warm potato salad or quickly sautéed cabbage, or slice thickly and serve with a tumble of sharply dressed green leaves or just a few dill pickles or cornichons. Unbelievably, you will need two bunches of spinach to make one cup of cooked spinach.

750 g (1½ lb) minced pork
6 slices prosciutto or pancetta, roughly chopped
250 g (9 oz) chicken livers, roughly chopped
1 cup cooked spinach, squeezed dry
1 tbsp thyme leaves
1 tbsp finely chopped sage leaves
1 garlic clove, crushed
1 onion, finely chopped
1 egg
salt and freshly ground black pepper
½ tsp cayenne pepper
½ tsp grated nutmeg
2 tbsp brandy or cognac
10 thin rashers rindless bacon

Mix minced pork, prosciutto, chicken livers, spinach, thyme, sage, garlic and onion in a large bowl, working them well with your hands. Add egg, salt, pepper, cayenne, nutmeg and brandy and continue to hand-mix until gooey.

Line a 1.5 litre (3 pint) terrine mould with bacon, leaving ends hanging over the edge. Fill terrine with meat mixture, and fold bacon ends back onto top. Seal with a sheet of silver foil tied with string, and place in a roasting pan. Pour boiling water to half way up the sides of the mould, and bake at 180°C (350°F) for 1½ hours, or until an inserted skewer comes out clean, and the sides have shrunk slightly away from the mould. Allow to cool for an hour or so, then weight lightly and leave to cool completely.

Serve at room temperature, or refrigerate for a day or two before serving.

Feeds eight to ten.

Spanakopita

It takes hundreds of years to ruin a dish like this, and we very nearly succeeded. That's the trouble with history. But I have always loved this eggy pie of spinach and feta in a thin shell of filo pastry, when freshly made and served still warm from the oven. The whole house fills with its wondrous smells as everyone tries to be civilised and not look too hungry. Filo pastry is easy to work with, as long as you do it quickly and don't expose it to too much air during preparation. And remember, you can't have enough spinach.

3 bunches spinach
2 tbsp olive oil
4 green (spring) onions, finely chopped
freshly ground black pepper
grated nutmeg
300 g (11 oz) feta cheese
4 eggs
1 tbsp finely chopped dill
1 packet filo pastry
125 g (4½ oz) melted butter

Heat oven to 180°C (350°F). Cut off any major stalks from the spinach and rinse the leaves well in a sink of cold water. Drain and chop roughly.

Heat olive oil in a pan and add spinach and green onions, tossing until wilted. Drain in a sieve or colander, then squeeze in your hands when cool, to get rid of excess juices. Mash feta cheese with a fork, beat in the eggs, dill and lots of pepper. Mix cheese with spinach, tossing well.

Cover filo pastry with a lightly damp, clean cloth, and lay out the top layer of pastry. Brush pastry with melted butter, and place in an lightly oiled ovenproof baking dish 24 cm by 28 cm (9½ by 11 in), allowing some pastry to overlap sides. Continue brushing pastry sheets with butter and laying into dish until you have 6 layers, then fill dish with spinach and cheese mixture and top with 6 more layers of buttered pastry, tucking in the edges.

Bake for 40 to 50 minutes, until the top is crisp and golden and the filling has set. Cool for 10 minutes or so, then cut into squares to serve.

Feeds four.

Pad Thai

This has to be the most morish, snacky noodle dish in the world, as your mouth goes on a roller-coaster ride from crunchy peanuts to little salty things to fresh bean shoots to soft noodles to garlicky chives and back again. It is much loved at every level of Thai society, from the streetside hawker with his bicycle and small gas burner, up.

150 g (5¼ oz) thin rice stick noodles
1½ tbsp tamarind pulp
3 tbsp boiling water
1½ tbsp palm sugar or brown sugar
3 tbsp oil
3 garlic cloves, finely chopped
3 tbsp dried shrimp, chopped
1 tbsp salted radish, chopped
1 tsp dried chilli flakes
2 tbsp fish sauce
2 cups bean shoots
2 eggs, lightly beaten
20 garlic chives, cut into 5 cm (2 in) lengths
2 tbsp hard beancurd, cubed
4 tbsp roasted peanuts, lightly crushed
2 or 3 coriander sprigs
1 lime, quartered

Soak rice stick noodles in cold water for 2 hours, then drain.

Combine tamarind, boiling water and sugar in a bowl. Stir until sugar dissolves. Leave to stand for 10 minutes or so, then strain off liquid and reserve.

Heat wok, then add 2 tablespoons of the oil. Add garlic, dried shrimp, radish and chilli, and fry for 2 minutes until garlic just turns golden. Add drained noodles and toss continually for 2 or 3 minutes. Add tamarind liquid and fish sauce, then all but a handful of bean shoots. Add the remaining tablespoon of oil. Move the noodles to one side of the wok and pour eggs into the space created, scrambling them roughly. Cover with noodles and toss through.

Add beancurd, garlic chives and the last handful of bean shoots and cook for a minute or two. Tip out onto a warm serving platter and scatter with crushed peanuts and coriander sprigs.

Serve with limes to squeeze over the top.

Feeds four.

Pan con tomate

You're going to thank me for this. It's one of the simplest and most popular accessories to a Catalan meal but it also makes the perfect lunch, topped with a slice of ham or some lush roasted red peppers (Pantry, 221), or served with a simple vegetable soup, or dipped into beans, or just crunched into when on the run.

4 soft bread rolls, preferably Spanish/Portuguese
4 tbsp fruity olive oil
2 garlic cloves, cut in half (optional)
4 ripe juicy tomatoes

Cut bread rolls in half lengthwise and lightly grill until warm.

Brush each slice with olive oil. Rub with a cut clove of garlic, if using. Cut each tomato in half, and rub the cut side of tomato over each slice, squeezing at the same time so the juices and seeds run out and are absorbed by the bread.

Return bread to the grill and heat until crisp at the edges.

Feeds four.

Rabbit rillettes

Known in my part of the woods as underground chicken, rabbit has a terrific flavour, especially when it is teamed with vegetables, herbs, spices, white wine and duck or goose fat in this rustic French paté. I would be sorry to see rabbits and their associated rural mythology go out of fashion and probably out of business. It is only recipes like this that will keep them on our table.

2 wild rabbits, jointed
1 tbsp rock salt or sea salt
1 tsp freshly ground black pepper
2 garlic cloves, smashed
4 sprigs of thyme
3 thick (1 cm or ½ in) slices speck or kaiserfleisch
2 carrots, peeled and chopped
2 bay leaves
3 parsley stalks
750 ml (one bottle) dry white wine
4 tbsp duck or goose fat or lard
1 extra bay leaf

Rub rabbits with salt, pepper, garlic and thyme. Place in a large bowl with speck or kaiserfleisch, carrots, bay leaves, parsley stalks and white wine, cover and chill overnight.

Remove rabbit and pork, and pat dry. Heat fat in a solid, flameproof casserole that is wide enough to lay rabbits in one layer. Cook rabbit and pork until lightly golden, about 10 minutes, turning often. Add marinade to the pan, until liquid just covers the meat. Bring to the boil, then lower heat and cook at a simmer, uncovered, for 3 or 4 hours, or until meat is falling off the bone.

Remove rabbit and pork from the pan, and shred the meat. Add salt and pepper to taste, bearing in mind rabbit has already been salted. Continue to simmer the cooking liquid if necessary, until reduced to one cup in volume. Strain the liquid, and pour over the shredded meat.

Pack meat into a porcelain bowl, pour a little extra melted fat on top to seal, set a bay leaf into the fat, cover and refrigerate overnight.

Serve with crusty French bread, a few cornichons (small green pickled gherkins) and a salad.

Feeds six.

Grilled seafood salad

A ridiculously easy dish for one so glamorous. Choose what leaps up at you at the fish shop – what is freshest and best – rather than slavishly following the recipe. This is brilliant served on top of a tangy, lemony tabbouleh salad (Salad, 76).

4 green tiger prawns
4 thick slices sour dough or pide bread
4 small fillets salmon
4 small fillets tuna
4 baby calamari tubes
1 lemon, quartered

Dressing
1 tbsp chopped fresh coriander
1 tbsp chopped fresh parsley
½ tsp paprika
sea salt and freshly ground black pepper
2 tbsp lemon juice
8 tbsp olive oil

Devein prawns by hooking out the dark intestinal tract with a fine bamboo skewer. Remove head and legs, and cut in half lengthwise, without cutting right through.

Mix coriander, parsley, paprika, salt, pepper, lemon juice and olive oil in a small bowl.

Heat grill, or use a lightly oiled cast-iron skillet on top of the stove. Brush bread with a little of the dressing and grill on both sides. Brush salmon, tuna, prawns and calamari with the dressing and grill lightly on both sides. Arrange on top of the grilled bread on each plate, with a lemon wedge. Drizzle with remaining dressing and serve.

Feeds four.

Dinner

As we go forward into the twenty-first century, so we go backward, to find what is real and true and what will last.

For dinner, that means slow roasts, fast grills, and heart-warming rice and grain dishes.

It doesn't mean garlic bread, nachos, deep-fried everything, or paper doilies.

Truffles and caviar are rather nice, but a good dinner doesn't need them.

We all want food that makes us feel comfortable, and warm and loved, and the time we want it is at the end of a hard day.

For this, we will conquer new worlds, fight impossible fights, work like galley slaves, and every now and then do the dishes and put out the garbage.

After all, that moment when you are ten minutes into eating your dinner should be the happiest moment of your entire day.

Dinner suggests generosity and plenty, Dickensian roasts, steaming hot pots, rosy-cheeked Rockwellian children, tablecloths, gleaming glasses, old oil paintings, laughter and music.

Dinner suggests meat and fish cooked on the bone, woks full of noodles, wooden spoons stirring pots of rice, corks easing out of bottles, crusty potato gratins, red wine sauces, steaming hot curries, and a savoury, spicy smell in the air.

Dinner also suggests a fast grill of skinny lamb chops, sweetly spiced sausages on a bed of cabbage, and sunny-coloured seafood paella.

Consider serving everything in the middle of the table on huge platters, rather than dividing things up on pretty little plates.

Cook as a couple, divvying up jobs like shopping and chopping.

While it soon becomes obvious that your taste and judgement are perfect while your partner's are questionable, dinner itself takes half the time.

Finally, there are two things you cannot do without at a fine dinner: candles and music.

Even when you are eating at the kitchen table with your shoes kicked off, there is no need to let yourself go.

Dinner

Poule au pot
Rib eye with caramelised onions
Tuscan roast chicken
Burger with blue cheese
Malaysian fish curry
Chilli salt prawns
B'stilla
Steamed fish with ginger
Corned beef with salsa verde
Cabbage rolls
Moussaka
Calves' liver with sweet onions
Seafood paella
Grilled lamb with lentils

Poule au pot

There is both a magnificence and a humility about this whole stuffed, poached chicken, served with vegetables in its own soupy juices, and I can't decide which sentiment is the more appealing. It has been the great middle-class dream ever since the good King Henry IV of Navarre wished that all his subjects might have a chicken in the pot (*poule au pot*) on every Sunday of the year.

1 free range chicken, size 16 or 18 (3 to 4 lb)
2 slices stale bread
½ cup milk
2 rashers bacon, finely diced
2 tbsp freshly chopped parsley
1 egg, lightly beaten
freshly grated nutmeg
250 g (9 oz) minced pork or chicken
6 medium carrots, peeled
2 turnips, peeled
4 smallish leeks, cleaned and trimmed
3 stalks celery
2 small onions, peeled
6 small potatoes, peeled
salt and freshly ground pepper
sprigs of fresh thyme and parsley

Soak bread in milk, then squeeze dry. Beat bread, bacon, parsley, egg, nutmeg and minced pork or chicken together with a wooden spoon, and stuff inside the cleaned and dried cavity of the chicken, sliding a little carefully between the skin and the breast as well.

Place in a large pot with carrots, turnips, leeks, celery, onion, potatoes, salt and pepper. Add boiling water to just cover the chicken, and bring to the boil, skimming to remove any icky stuff that floats to the surface. Reduce to a gentle simmer, cover, and leave to simmer for 1½ hours.

Remove chicken from pot, and carve into large, generous pieces. Arrange vegetables on a large, warmed serving dish, and lay chicken pieces on top. Spoon over enough of the stock to moisten well. Tuck in the thyme and parsley, and take to the table.

Serve in shallow pasta bowls with a few spoonfuls of broth.

Feeds four to six.

Rib eye with caramelised onions

The large, marbled, standing rib roast of aged beef is almost a thing of the past. This recipe revives it in spirit at least, although cooked – in the modern way – for individuals. As always, the trick is going to the best butcher possible, and paying for quality. Serve with perfect mash (Potatoes, 116) or celeriac purée (Vegetables, 128).

2 tbsp olive oil
1 tbsp butter
1 kg (2 lb) small onions, peeled
1 tsp brown sugar
2 beef rib eyes on bone, well aged
freshly cracked black pepper
1 tbsp olive oil
1 garlic clove, smashed

Heat olive oil and butter in a heavy-bottomed frypan. Add onions and toss well. Sprinkle with sugar and cook, shaking the pan occasionally, for an hour, until golden brown, sweet and soft.

Rub beef with a little cracked black pepper. Heat oil and garlic in a heavy-based frypan and sear beef for a few minutes on all sides until crusty and brown. Place in the oven and roast for 15 minutes at 190°C (375°F). Remove and allow to rest for 10 minutes in a warm place before serving.

Place mashed potato or celeriac purée in centre of each plate. Top with beef rib eye and a ladleful of caramelised onions, or carve the meat in thick slices from the bone, and serve with a great red wine.

Feeds two, magnificently.

Tuscan roast chicken

Tuscan cooking was the essence of simplicity long before minimalism became a fashion. Golden roast chicken and a nutty, creamy split pea purée are linked with a ribbon of Tuscan olive oil. Resist the impulse to add any garnish, any sauce, or any sundried tomato, and leave the lily ungilded.

1 free range chicken, jointed
3 tbsp olive oil
1 tbsp lemon juice
sprigs of rosemary
sprigs of sage
sea salt and pepper

Split pea purée
400 g (14 oz) dried yellow split peas
4 cups water
2 tbsp olive oil
1 onion, finely chopped
sea salt and pepper
2 tbsp extra virgin olive oil

Wash and dry chicken pieces and arrange in a large bowl. Add olive oil, lemon juice, rosemary, sage, salt and pepper and toss with your hands until well coated. Leave to marinate for an hour or two.

Rinse split peas under cold running water. Place in a pot with water and bring to the boil. Skim off any froth, then reduce heat and add olive oil, onion and salt. Cover and simmer for 1½ to 2 hours, without stirring, until the peas form a thick purée. Beat peas with a wooden spoon to amalgamate into a paste. Add salt and pepper to taste, and keep warm.

Heat oven to 200°C (400°F). Pour any remaining marinade into a heavy-bottomed frypan and fry the chicken in 2 batches until golden. Arrange chicken in a baking pan. Place pan in oven and roast for around 15 minutes until skin is golden brown and meat is tender and cooked through.

Serve on a bed of split pea purée with a drizzle of extra virgin olive oil.

Feeds four.

Burger with blue cheese

The burger as we know it first appeared on the menu of New York's famous Delmonico's restaurant in 1934. In spite of its sorry image, it is a legitimate, honest meal that should be brought back into the fold of good home cooking as soon as possible. The beetroot is optional (mandatory for Australians).

1 tbsp light olive oil
1 onion, finely chopped
2 red peppers (capsicums)
2 slices white bread
½ cup milk
750 g (1½ lb) quality minced beef (e.g. rump)
1 tbsp finely chopped parsley
1 tbsp finely snipped chives
sea salt and freshly ground pepper
1 egg, lightly beaten
½ cup blue cheese
4 tbsp quality mayonnaise
4 slices pancetta or bacon
extra tbsp olive oil
handful of rocket leaves
4 sourdough rolls, focaccia or muffins
1 fresh beetroot, cooked (optional)

Heat olive oil and cook onion until it softens, then set aside. Bake peppers in moderate oven for 30 minutes until they darken. Let cool, and peel off skins. Cut in half lengthwise, discard seeds, and trim into 4 pieces. Slice trimmings into strips and set aside.

Soak white bread in milk, and squeeze dry and finely chop. Mix minced beef, bread, herbs, salt and pepper in a large bowl. Add egg, and mix well with your hands, squeezing and kneading. Form into four large patties, cover with plastic wrap and chill until needed.

Mash blue cheese, mix with mayonnaise and chill. Grill pancetta or bacon, and lightly toast halved rolls. Heat extra olive oil in heavy-based frypan and cook burgers for 3 or 4 minutes on either side, depending on thickness.

To assemble, place rocket leaves on a toasted half bun. Top with roasted red pepper, burger, beetroot (optional), pancetta or bacon, red pepper strips and a dollop of blue cheese mayonnaise.

Feeds four.

Malaysian fish curry

If this book was scratch 'n' sniff, you'd be rushing off to cook this now, unable to hold out. Known as ikan gulai (*ikan* is fish and *gulai* is a thin curry traditionally made by the *nonya*, the Straits-born women of Malaysia), it's a spice odyssey through coriander, cumin, fish-loving fennel seed and turmeric, smoothed with coconut milk and soured with tamarind. Bet you can smell it anyway.

500 g (1lb) firm fish steaks e.g. ling, cod, snapper
1½ tbsp tamarind pulp
½ cup boiling water
1 peeled white stalk of lemon grass, sliced
4 dried red chillies, soaked and drained
1 tbsp freshly grated ginger
2 garlic cloves
8 shallots or 1 onion, chopped
2 tbsp vegetable oil
1 tbsp ground coriander
1 tsp ground cumin
1 tsp ground fennel
1 tsp ground turmeric
6 curry leaves
1 tsp salt
1 tsp sugar
1 cup coconut milk

Remove any skin or bones from fish and cut into bite-sized pieces. Soak tamarind pulp in boiling water and leave for 10 minutes, then knead to dissolve. Strain, and set tamarind water aside.

Grind, pound or blend lemon grass, drained chillies, ginger, garlic and shallots or onion to a paste.

Heat oil in wok or frypan and fry paste for 5 minutes, stirring, until it smells fragrant. Add coriander, cumin, fennel, turmeric, curry leaves, salt and sugar, then slowly add coconut milk, stirring. Bring up to the boil, stirring constantly. Add tamarind water and simmer for 10 minutes, stirring occasionally, until the sauce thickens slightly, uncovered. Add fish, and simmer for 3 minutes until just cooked.

Serve with stir-fried green beans or water spinach (kang kong), and lots of rice.

Feeds four.

Chilli salt prawns

Fly to Hong Kong, jump on a ferry and choof off to Lamma Island, where you can sit at a seaside seafood restaurant and nibble these wok-tossed prawns coated in chilli salt to your heart's content. Or just fly to the fish shop, jump into your kitchen, and choof off to the table. Less frequent flyer points, but more fun.

12 medium or 20 small fresh raw prawns
1 tbsp grated ginger
2 tbsp Chinese rice wine or dry sherry
1 tbsp sea salt
2 garlic cloves, crushed
2 red chillies, finely sliced (optional)

Devein prawns by hooking out the black intestinal tract with a thin bamboo skewer, leaving prawns in their shells. Place in a shallow heat-proof bowl with grated ginger and rice wine and rub to coat the shells. Leave for one hour, tossing occasionally.

Transfer bowl to steamer and steam over simmering water for 5 minutes, or until prawn meat turns white. Remove and drain, and dry prawns with paper towel.

Heat wok with salt, garlic and chilli (no oil) over medium heat. Add prawns and toss until hot and well coated with salt.

Serve with soy dipping sauce (Broths and Sauces, 206) and plenty of steamed jasmine rice.

Feeds four.

B'stilla

B'stilla is an extraordinary Moroccan pie of lemony chicken and herbs encased in filo pastry and dusted with sweet, seductive cinnamon and icing sugar. The original version is rich and heavy with butter, but I have lightened it considerably. The chic stencilled pattern of cinnamon and icing sugar is done through a good old-fashioned paper doily, but don't tell anyone, and they'll think you trained in Marrakesh.

4 chicken thighs
4 chicken drumsticks
1 quantity chermoula marinade (Pantry, 218)
1 litre (1¾ pints) boiling water
1 tsp saffron, powdered
1 tbsp chopped parsley
1 tsp grated lemon rind
2 tbsp icing sugar
2 tbsp ground cinnamon
2 tbsp ground almonds
1 packet filo pastry
3 tbsp melted butter for filo pastry

Rub chicken pieces with chermoula, and leave to marinate overnight. Transfer chicken and chermoula to a large pot and add boiling water and saffron. Cover and simmer for one hour, skimming occasionally, until chicken is tender. Strain liquid into a saucepan and boil until liquid is reduced to around ¾ cup. Allow chicken to cool, then shred it with your fingers, discarding bones and skin.

Mix chicken, parsley, lemon rind and reduced liquid, and set aside. Mix icing sugar, cinnamon and ground almonds and set aside.

Heat oven to 180°C (350°F). Brush one sheet of filo pastry with melted butter, lay another sheet on top, brush it with melted butter and continue until you have 6 sheets. Dust with a little of the icing sugar mixture. Place chicken mixture on top, and fold the pastry over the chicken. Dust with more icing sugar mixture, then place 2 more buttered sheets of filo on top, tucking in the edges, to encase the entire pie. Place on a baking tray, baste with melted butter and bake for 30 minutes, until pastry is golden and filling is hot. Remove from oven and slide onto warmed serving plate.

Dust with icing sugar and cinnamon, through a doily if you admit to having one, and serve at the table, cut into wedges.

Feeds four.

Steamed fish with ginger

Until steamers come fish-shaped, confine your steaming to plate-sized fish, or you'll have serious trouble with heads and tails. This classic Chinese method is surely the finest way to cook fish in all the world, and one of the healthiest. It would pay to invest in a double-decker steamer from Chinatown, if you want to cook four fish at a time.

4 plate-sized snapper, bream, or baby salmon, around 400g (14 oz each)
several lettuce or cabbage leaves
4 tbsp soy sauce
1 tbsp sesame oil
2 tbsp Chinese rice wine
1 tbsp sugar
5 cm (2 in) knob of ginger
1 small red chilli, sliced (optional)
3 green (spring) onions, finely chopped
5 tbsp peanut oil
half a bunch of coriander

Scale, clean and gut fish. Wash and dry well. Use a sharp knife to make three slashes in the thickest part of the fish, on both sides.

Fill base of steamer with water and bring to the boil. Line 2 shallow heat-proof bowls with leaves and lay fish on top of leaves. Mix soy, sesame oil, rice wine and sugar, and pour on top. Peel ginger and cut into tiny matchsticks. Scatter ginger, chilli and half the spring onions on top of fish and place in the steamer. Steam for 12 to 15 minutes, but start checking at around 10 minutes to see how fish is doing: the flesh should part easily from the bone when pierced with a knife. Remove fish from steamer when cooked.

Heat peanut oil in a small pan until it just starts to smoke. Remove fish from steamer and pour the hot oil on top of the fish. The skin will crackle and sizzle, and the oil will add to the cooking juices to make a wonderful, aromatic sauce. Top with remaining spring onions and coriander leaves and serve with jasmine rice.

To serve, run a sharp knife through the flesh from head to tail, then cut across into 3 sections. Distribute among four Chinese serving plates, then turn fish over and repeat the exercise. Don't forget to drench your rice with the cooking juices.

Feeds four.

Corned beef with salsa verde

I've traded recipes for this good old Anglo corned beef (silverside) with supermarket millionaires and taxi drivers, and I still cook it every time I come home from an extended trip out of the country. The only dilemma is whether to make it with a sharp salsa verde, or a light parsley sauce (see cheese sauce, Broths and Sauces, 209). I serve it like this the first night, and the other way the next.

1.5 kg (3 lb) piece corned beef (brisket/silverside)
3 onions, peeled
3 carrots, peeled and chopped
2 celery stalks, chopped
1 bay leaf

Salsa verde
1 cup flat-leafed parsley
1 cup fresh basil
1 cup mint leaves
1 garlic clove, crushed
2 tbsp tiny salted capers, rinsed
4 anchovies, rinsed
freshly ground black pepper
2 tbsp red wine vinegar
6 tbsp or more of extra virgin olive oil

Rinse beef, place in a big pot with lots of cold water and bring to the boil. Reduce to a simmer, skimming off any froth. Add onions, carrots, celery and bay leaf and cook slowly, partly covered, for around 2 hours at a bare simmer. Remove from heat, although beef can stay in broth for a few hours until ready to reheat.

Wash parsley, basil and mint, and shake dry. Combine herbs in food processor and chop until fine using the pulse action. Add garlic, capers, and anchovies and chop until fine. Keep the motor running while you add the vinegar, then, more slowly, the olive oil. Taste for pepper and adjust accordingly and set aside, covered.

Reheat broth and corned beef gently. Remove beef from the broth and drain. Slice the beef and arrange on warmed serving plates. Spoon the salsa verde on top, and serve.

Feeds six.

Cabbage rolls

Strangely but truly, cabbages were originally grown for their stems, until the Romans cultivated cabbage with larger, more developed heads in Caesar's time. The Romans also swore that eating cabbage during a banquet would keep you from getting drunk. I tried it. It doesn't work.

1 large cabbage
1 tsp salt
2 slices stale country bread, crusts removed
½ cup milk
500 g (1 lb) minced pork or sausage meat
½ cup raw rice
½ onion, grated
1 garlic clove, crushed
2 tbsp chopped parsley
1 tsp paprika
sea salt and freshly ground black pepper
500 ml (18 fl oz) tomato and basil sauce
  (Broths and Sauces, 210)
1 cup sour cream for serving (optional)

Discard tough outer leaves from cabbage and cut out the tough central core. Cook in a large pot of simmering, salted water for 5 to 10 minutes, then remove cabbage, reserving water, and rinse well under cold water. Peel off the leaves and pat dry. Cut out any thick stem and trim into 8 rough circles of around 20 cm (8 in) diameter.

Soak bread in milk, then squeeze dry. Mix meat with rice, grated onion, garlic, parsley, bread, paprika, salt and pepper with your hands. Lay out one circle of cabbage, and top with a handful of meat mixture. Roll up as if for a spring roll, tucking in the edges as you go (the first one is messy, then you'll get the hang of it). Arrange rolls, tightly packed, in a flat-bottomed pan, and enough of the reserved cabbage cooking water to just cover. Simmer gently for 1 hour, covered.

Heat tomato sauce and warm six shallow soup or pasta plates. Remove cabbage rolls from liquid, drain, and place one roll on each serving plate. Spoon hot tomato sauce around each one and serve with sour cream if you are feeling very European.

Feeds four to six.

Moussaka

Here's blasphemy for you. I've deconstructed the traditional – and usually heavy and oily – Greek layered and slow-baked dish of lamb, béchamel sauce and eggplant, and turned it into a lighter, faster moussaka by going vertical instead of horizontal. Try it first, before you damn my soul to hell for mucking around with the classics.

3 medium eggplants (aubergines)
fine grained salt
2 tbsp olive oil
1 onion, finely chopped
1 garlic clove, crushed
500 g (1 lb) lean minced lamb
½ cup white wine
1 cup tomato passato (purée)
1 tbsp tomato paste (concentrate)
1 tbsp finely chopped fresh parsley
1 tsp fresh chopped oregano
sea salt and freshly ground black pepper
2 tbsp olive oil
½ tsp ground cinnamon
1 quantity cheese sauce (Broths and Sauces, 209)

Cut eggplant into twelve 1 cm (½ in) thick slices, sprinkle with salt, and leave on a tray for 2 hours. Rinse and pat dry with paper towel to remove any bitter juices and salt.

Heat olive oil and cook onion and garlic for 10 minutes. Add meat and brown well. Add white wine, tomato passato, tomato paste, parsley, oregano, salt and pepper, bring to the boil, then simmer for 30 minutes.

Heat olive oil in a large frypan and fry each slice of eggplant on both sides until golden brown, or brush with olive oil and grill on or under a hot grill. Keep warm.

Make the cheese sauce and keep warm.

To assemble, place one eggplant slice in the centre of each warmed plate, top with a spoonful of minced lamb and a spoonful of cheese sauce, then another slice of eggplant, a spoonful of meat, then of cheese sauce, and top with the smallest, crispest slices of eggplant. Serve immediately.

Feeds four.

Calves' liver with sweet onions

Those who go 'eergh' and turn the page haven't tasted the classic Venetian combination of thinly sliced calves' liver and sweet melting onions. Tradition dictates the liver is cooked with the onions, but I prefer to sear it quickly in a separate pan. Calves' liver is relatively cheap, so buy more than you need, and trim it well into large pieces that are easy to slice.

1 kg (2 lb) calves' liver
3 tbsp butter
2 cups dry white wine
1 kg (2 lb) onions, finely sliced
salt and freshly ground black pepper
125 ml (4 fl oz) chicken broth or water
1 tbsp butter
1 tbsp light olive oil
4 sprigs of sage
4 sprigs of rosemary

Remove any membrane or icky bits from liver and cut into extremely thin slices.

Heat butter, wine and onions in a heavy-bottomed pan and cook, covered, over a low heat for 45 minutes, stirring occasionally, until onion is almost melting. Add salt and pepper to taste, and a little chicken broth or water if needed, to keep it moist and creamy. If too moist, remove cover and cook over high heat for a minute or two.

Heat butter and oil in a heavy-bottomed pan and add half the sage and rosemary leaves, to flavour the oil. Cook liver over very high heat, tossing well, for no more than 30 seconds; so it is almost crusty outside, and pink inside.

Divide onion sauce between plates, and top with liver, piled high. Add fresh sage and rosemary, and serve.

Feeds four.

Seafood paella

Paella is a family – even community – Spanish dish, originally eaten outside, cooked over hot coals on a *paella*, a wide, flat pan that allows plenty of surface contact with the heat, and the smoke to curl itself over the edge and imbue the rice with its magic. It is also traditionally cooked by the men of the household, a fact that some women resent, although smart women seem to think it is a damn good idea.

2 pinches saffron threads or good quality saffron powder
1 tsp Spanish paprika
1 red pepper (capsicum)
3 tbsp olive oil
½ whole head of garlic, cut crosswise
1 onion, finely chopped
3 tomatoes, roughly chopped
500 g (1 lb) short grain arborio rice
1 thick slice cooked ham, finely chopped
green beans, blanched
salt and freshly ground black pepper
1.5 litres (3 pints) chicken broth or water, boiling
8 medium green (raw) prawns, deveined
500 g (1 lb) clams or mussels, prepared (Pantry, 217)
4 small calamari, cleaned and cut into rings

Dissolve saffron in a little boiling water or stock, add paprika, and set aside. Cut red pepper in half, remove seeds and cut flesh into short strips.

Heat oil in your largest, widest pan (around 40 cm or 16 in in diameter) with the shallowest sides, over two burners if necessary. Add the garlic half, cut side down. Add onion and cook gently until soft. Add chopped tomatoes and red pepper and cook for 5 minutes. Add rice and cook gently for 5 minutes until well coated. Add ham, green beans, salt and pepper, saffron and paprika water, and boiling water or broth, and bring to the boil, stirring. Stop stirring and simmer very gently, uncovered, for 20 minutes, moving the dish around on the heat occasionally.

Arrange prawns on top of rice, pushing them in slightly. Add mussels or clams, prepared and partly cooked as on page 217. Top with calamari, cover with a lid or silver foil, and continue to cook gently for 10 to 15 minutes by which time the rice should be very nearly cooked and tender. Add extra broth or water if the rice seems dry, but do not stir.

Remove from the heat and leave to rest for 5 minutes before serving straight from the pan.

Feeds four to six.

Grilled lamb with lentils

Grilled lamb chops have been a favourite meal since I was old enough to hold a bone. That's what comes of growing up on a sheep farm. These days, I like them well trimmed (I buy trimmed racks of lamb and chop them myself) and cooked fast and rare, served with plump, juicy lentils or, if I'm regressing, mashed potatoes and a million peas.

2 tbsp olive oil
1 onion, finely chopped
1 garlic clove, crushed
1 tomato, finely chopped
300 g (11 oz) brown lentils, rinsed
2 six-bone racks of young lamb
3 tbsp finely chopped parsley
3 tbsp extra virgin olive oil
sea salt and freshly ground black pepper

Heat olive oil and add onion and garlic. Cook gently, stirring, for 10 minutes until soft. Add tomato and cook for 5 minutes. Add lentils, and pour in boiling water to cover lentils by about 3 cm (1¼ in). Cook gently for 20 to 30 minutes until tender, topping up water if necessary.

Heat grill until very hot. Cut racks into individual chops, and trim well. Place chops on grill and leave without moving for 2 minutes until strongly marked. Turn and cook the other side, again without moving them around the grill.

Drain off any water the lentils haven't yet absorbed, and stir in parsley, olive oil and sea salt and pepper to taste. Spoon lentils on warmed dinner plates, and stack lamb chops on top. Top with a tangy salsa verde (page 45) if desired.

Feeds four.

Cocktails

Drink whatever is in fashion.
Over a normal life span, you will then try everything at least once.
Or just stick to the very best cocktails, which are, of course, the oldest – the classic dry martini, the salt-crusted margarita.
Add the Bellini, created in the 1930s by Giuseppe Cipriani, father of Arrigo and founder of the world's most perfect bar, Harry's Bar in Venice.
It was eventually named in 1948 in honour of the Italian artist Giovanni Bellini.
And add the bicicletta, brought to Australia by inspired restaurateur Maurizio Terzini from his spiritual home, the *bacari*, or wine bars, of Venice.
It is unbelievably, irrevocably, irreparably chic, and I have no idea why it is called a bicicletta.
Or maybe I have forgotten.
It happens, when you drink cocktails.
As for the dry martini, you can forget James Bond.
A classic martini should be stirred with ice then strained. If shaken, it will appear cloudy.
The original Martini cocktail – first known in America in the 1860s and possibly created by a bartender known as Martinez – called for two parts gin to one part vermouth, but a drier version has since become the classic.
If you like it drier, just rinse the glass with the vermouth and tip it out.
If you like it colder, keep your gin and vermouth in the refrigerator.
The salt crusted glass of the classic Margarita is a reference to the traditional Mexican tequila-drinking ritual in which one holds a quarter of lime in the left hand, and places a little well of salt in the pouch of skin between thumb and forefinger.
You lick the salt with your tongue, drink the tequila held in your other hand, then suck the lime.
It's not very elegant, which is why they created the Margarita.
Speaking of elegance, please make sure the lid of the cocktail shaker is properly on, before you start to shake.

Bellini
Chill glasses.
Skin 6 ripe white peaches.
Squeeze each peach between your hands over a bowl, catching all juices and pulp.
Push flesh and juices through a sieve, using a wooden spoon.
Chill peach juice until ready to serve.
Chill 750 ml (26 fl oz) Prosecco, or any good sparkling dry wine.
Combine one part peach juice to three or four parts well chilled Prosecco.
Add a dash of chilled Cointreau, if the peaches are a little tart. Makes six.

Bicicletta
Chill a tall glass.
Add ice and pour 40 ml (1½ fl oz) Campari over ice.
Add a healthy dash of Pinot Grigio, dry Italian white wine.
Top with soda water. Serves one.

Dry martini
Chill a classic dry martini glass by dipping it gently in crushed ice and rolling it.
Rub the rim of the glass with the cut edge of a strip of lemon peel.
Pour 100 ml (3½ fl oz) good gin (e.g. Gordon's) over ice, add 10 ml (⅓ fl oz) good vermouth (e.g. Noilly Prat) and stir.
Strain quickly into glass.
Add either one green olive spiked on a toothpick, or the twist of lemon peel. Serves one.

Margarita
Chill a large martini glass.
Wet the rim of the glass by rubbing it with a wedge of lime.
Dip rim in a saucer of salt.
Shake off excess.
Shake 3 tbsp gold Tequila, 1 tbsp Cointreau or Triple Sec, 2 tbsp fresh lime juice
and 1 tsp egg white with ice blocks in a shaker.
Shake vigorously, then strain carefully into glass, avoiding the salt rim. Serves one.

Soups are just water with added value.

But they are far from humble.

Soups are the noble voices of distinctly different countries in liquid form; steaming bowls of symbolism; spoonfuls of culture, to be sipped and swallowed.

Soups come from what is in season, and from a long tradition of 'making do'.

Soup is simple, natural, functional, and full of common sense.

You know how mothers and grandmothers insist that soup wards off colds and flu?

Well, of course it does, because you stay at home in order to eat their soup, instead of whipping out in the wind and rain to buy some pathetic form of take-out food.

Even medical science hasn't come up with a better cure for the common cold than not catching it in the first place.

With a pot of soup on the stove, you are socially secure. Anything could happen, and you would rise to the occasion.

But the real reason we should cook soup at home is because we can.

Restaurants can't. They can do rich bisque, fancy crème soups and clarified consommés, but only we can do the sort of soup we want when we want soup.

And the nicest thing about them is that they are just as good to make as they are to eat.

Cook up a chicken soup every Saturday to sustain you for the week ahead.

Make a fresh vegetable soup every Sunday night, with anything left lying around the refrigerator:

cabbage, potatoes and celery leaves; peas and lettuce leaves; pumpkin and parsnip; mushrooms and rice;

ham hocks and beans; or carrots and cream.

The word comes from the ancient French 'sop', a hunk of bread over which broth was poured to make a hearty meal; still a great way to serve it.

So make soup.

Until we find a cure for the common cold, or for clinical depression, or for jamming your finger in a cupboard door, soup is all we have to make ourselves feel better.

Soup

Acquacotta
Oyster and leek chowder
Sopa de tortilla
French carrot soup
Chicken noodle soup
Green pea and lettuce soup
Orange soup
Fresh tomato soup
Sichuan hot and sour soup
Venetian bean soup
Zuppa alla Pavese
Won ton soup

Acquacotta

Acqua is Italian for water and cotta is Italian for cooked; a perfect description of normal soup, but completely libellous and misleading when it comes to the rich bright flavours of this traditional Tuscan soup. The vegetables are cooked in fruity olive oil, the boiling water releases their flavour, and the whole thing is enriched with eggs at the last minute. It looks a bit murky once the eggs go in, but the flavour is wonderful.

4 thick slices of sourdough bread
2 tbsp olive oil
2 onions, sliced into rings
1 red pepper (capsicum)
3 celery stalks, finely chopped
500 g (1 lb) canned tomatoes with juices
6 cups boiling water
sea salt and freshly ground pepper
2 eggs
2 tbsp grated Parmigiano cheese
2 tbsp extra virgin olive oil

Toast the bread ahead of time and allow to cool.

Heat the oil in a large frypan and cook onions until soft. Cut red pepper in half, remove seeds and cut into thin strips. Add celery, red pepper and tomatoes to pan. Cook for 30 minutes until soft. Add boiling water, salt and pepper, and cook for 10 minutes until soup is rich and thick.

Place grilled bread in soup bowls and drizzle with olive oil. Beat eggs, cheese, salt and pepper together, and add to soup, stirring. Remove from the heat immediately, and keep stirring until eggs are cooked through the soup.

Pour soup over toast, and serve with extra grated Parmigiano.

Feeds four.

Oyster and leek chowder

When oysters were cheap, even the poor would toss dozens of them into soups like this, though they may have had to save up for the potato with which to thicken it. Now it's the other way around. If you're feeling particularly poor, call it potato and leek chowder instead. Even without the oysters, it has a rich, luxurious taste.

1 dozen oysters
6 leeks, white parts only
3 tbsp butter
4 red-skinned potatoes
1 litre (1¾ pints) chicken broth
salt
freshly ground black pepper
freshly grated nutmeg
3 tbsp running cream

Open oysters and pour off all juices into a small bowl. Remove oysters from shells and set aside. Strain oyster juices through damp, fine muslin and set aside.

Wash leeks carefully, and cut into 1 cm (½ in) lengths. Melt butter in a large pan, add leeks and cook gently until they soften. Peel and slice potatoes, and add to leeks with chicken broth. Bring to the boil, then reduce heat to a simmer. Simmer gently until all vegetables are soft. Add salt, pepper and nutmeg to taste. Blend in a food processor, or force through a fine sieve or food mill.

Return to a clean saucepan and heat. Just before serving, add cream and oyster juices and taste for salt and pepper. Divide oysters among lightly warmed soup bowls, and top with soup.

Feeds four.

Sopa de tortilla

For centuries, Mexico has harvested golden ears of corn, grinding the kernels into a dough called masa, the base for tortillas, the 'bread' of Mexico. This classic Mexican soup combines chilli, tomato, avocado, and a hit of lime, and is topped with a frizz of crisp fried tortilla strips.

2 garlic cloves, peeled
1 onion, cut into four
4 tomatoes, cut in half
2 tbsp oil
6 to 8 cups chicken broth, hot
½ tsp ground, roasted cumin seeds
½ tsp salt
2 dried pasilla chillies or 1 tsp chilli powder
salt and freshly ground pepper
8 corn tortillas, a day old
3 tbsp oil for frying
1 avocado, peeled, stoned and sliced
2 tbsp fetta or cheddar cheese, crumbled
2 limes, cut in half

Place garlic cloves, onion and tomatoes in roasting pan. Bake at 180°C (350°F) for 20 to 30 minutes until soft and coloured. Whizz in food processor until smooth.

Heat oil in frypan, and add tomato purée and cook, stirring for around 5 minutes until it starts to thicken.

Add chicken broth in a saucepan and bring to the boil, stirring. Add ground cumin and salt. Reduce heat and simmer for 15 minutes, stirring occasionally.

Roast chillies in a dry pan until smoky but not blackened. Crush into pieces and set aside. Cut tortillas into thin strips, using a pair of scissors. Heat oil in a small frypan. Add tortilla strips a few at a time, and fry until crisp. Drain well.

Divide soup among warm bowls. Top with sliced avocado, crumbled cheese and crushed chillies. Pile crisp fried tortilla strips on top and serve with cut limes on the side.

Feeds four.

French carrot soup

The classic French potage Crécy, named for the carrot-growing Crécy area in the Ile de France that surrounds Paris. Here it is thickened with rice, but you could happily add three or four finely chopped potatoes instead, which will make it just as creamy and satisfying. A little butter swirled in at the end is traditional.

2 tbsp butter
8 medium carrots, peeled and sliced
1 onion, chopped
5 cups boiling water or chicken broth
3 tbsp rice, washed
sea salt and freshly ground pepper
1 extra tsp butter
1 tbsp finely chopped chervil

Melt butter and toss carrots and onions until coated. Cover and cook gently for 10 minutes, adding a little water if necessary. Add boiling water or broth, and rice. Cover and cook for 20 minutes.

Whizz in the food processor or put through a food mill until smooth. Return the purée to pan and reheat, tasting for salt and pepper. Add butter, divide among serving bowls and top with chervil.

Feeds four.

Chicken noodle soup

The secret to Jewish chicken soup is to use an old boiling hen and to skim a lot. And, probably, to be Jewish. Serve with lokshen (noodles) on the Sabbath if you are orthodox, and any time if you are not. The very best secret, of course, is to have your own chicken in the backyard.

1 large boiling chicken, cleaned
2 carrots, peeled
1 parsnip, peeled
3 celery stalks
2 leeks
3 parsley stalks
salt and freshly ground black pepper
200 g (7 oz) thin egg noodles, broken up
2 tbsp finely chopped parsley

Place chicken in a large pot. Add cold water until the chicken is just covered, and bring to the boil. Skim well to remove any froth that rises to the surface. Chop carrots, parsnip, leeks and celery. Wash leeks well in a bowl of cold water and drain. Add vegetables to pot with parsley stalks. Simmer, covered, for 45 minutes, then remove chicken. Remove breasts from chicken and set aside, moistened with a little broth.

Return carcass to broth and simmer for 2 hours.

Strain soup and simmer until volume is reduced to around 8 cups. At this point, you can slice the chicken breast, use the meat in the soup, or serve the meat as a second course. Add noodles and cook for a few minutes until tender.

Divide soup between 4 warmed soup bowls, and scatter parsley on top.

Feeds four.

Green pea and lettuce soup

A very sophisticated pea and lettuce soup known as potage Saint-Germain, named for the Comte de Saint-Germain, war minister under Louis XV, and probably created to celebrate the relatively new concept of fresh green peas. I've added a bunch of spinach for extra brightness of colour and flavour, and because I like spinach.

4 leeks
1 bunch spinach
2 tbsp butter
sea salt and freshly ground black pepper
2 cups green peas, podded
head of butter lettuce, outer leaves removed
1 tbsp sugar
1.5 litres (3 pints) water or chicken broth
1 tbsp chopped parsley
1 tbsp chopped chervil
1 tbsp butter

Trim tops off leeks, cut into thick slices, and rinse well. Drain and set aside. Wash spinach leaves in a big pot of cold water and rinse gently under cold running water. Drain and set to one side.

Heat butter, add leeks, salt and pepper. Cook gently for 20 minutes until soft. Add spinach leaves, peas, lettuce, sugar and broth or water. Cook for 15 minutes or until peas are tender. Whizz in food processor or food mill with parsley and chervil.

Return to heat, whisk in butter and serve.

Feeds four.

Orange soup

A fresh, tangy, citrus soup from the Dominican Republic that makes use of the island's fresh oranges. Serve chilled on a hot summer's day as an edible aperitif, and follow with grilled fish and vegetable salads. I think of this as more of a fruit cocktail than a soup, which gets around my prejudice against chilled soups.

4 cups chicken broth
grated rind of one large orange
2 cinnamon sticks
4 cloves
salt
2 cups freshly squeezed orange juice
1 dash Tabasco or chilli sauce
1 medium orange, finely sliced
1 fresh red chilli, sliced

Bring the broth to the boil. Add orange rind, cinnamon sticks, cloves and salt. Simmer for 15 minutes. Add orange juice and Tabasco and bring quickly to the boil, stirring. Remove from the heat as soon as it comes to the boil, and let cool. Strain and chill.

Serve in small or shallow soup bowls with ice blocks. Float orange slices and a slice of chilli on top.

Feeds four.

Fresh tomato soup

This recipe must have been the original version, before they thought to can it. If you like, you can whizz it in the blender, put it through a food mill, or best of all, leave it in its natural, smashed-up state. If your tomatoes aren't summer-ripe and juicy, add a spoonful of tomato paste with the broth or water.

2 tbsp olive oil
2 garlic cloves, smashed
2 onions, sliced into rings
1 kg (2 lb) ripe tomatoes
2 litres (3½ pints) vegetable broth or water
sea salt and freshly ground black pepper
20 fresh basil leaves
1 tbsp finely chopped parsley

Heat oil in frypan and gently cook onion and garlic for 30 minutes, until soft and sweet. Fish out the garlic and discard. Cut tomatoes in half, squeeze out seeds and juice, and chop the flesh roughly. Add tomatoes to onion and cook for five minutes over high heat. Add vegetable broth or water and bring to the boil. Simmer for 5 minutes. Taste for salt and pepper and adjust flavour. Return to pan and add basil and parsley. Whizz very briefly in food processor or food mill.

Serve in warmed soup bowls, with crusty bread.

Feeds four.

Sichuan hot and sour soup

If you have ever been in Sichuan in winter, you will understand the need for this soup. With its lusty vinegar sharpness and warm peppery heat, it's like lighting a blazing fire from within. Sichuan peppercorns (fagara), the tiny berries of the prickly ash tree, and Sichuan preserved vegetables can be found at Asian food stores.

100 g (3½ oz) pork fillet
½ tsp salt
2 tsp cornflour
4 Chinese mushrooms, soaked
2 tbsp bamboo shoots
1 beancurd cake
1 green (spring) onion
1 slice ginger
2 tbsp Sichuan preserved vegetables
2 tbsp wood-ear fungus, soaked
1 litre (1¾ pints) chicken broth
1 tbsp soy sauce
2 tbsp vinegar
1 tsp salt
1 tbsp cornflour, mixed with 2 tbsp cold water
2 eggs
1 tsp sesame oil
1 tsp Sichuan peppercorns, ground
1 tbsp coriander, finely chopped

Cut pork into thin matchstick shreds and mix with salt and cornflour. Cut mushrooms, bamboo shoots, beancurd, green onion, ginger, vegetables and fungus into the same size matchstick strips.

Bring broth to the boil. Add pork and all sliced ingredients. Cook for 2 minutes. Add soy sauce, vinegar, salt and cornflour mixture. Keep the broth at a gentle bubble, and stir well.

Beat the eggs in a small bowl, then pour very slowly into the bubbling soup through the tines of a fork. Remove from heat, add sesame oil, pepper, and coriander. Taste, and adjust vinegar and pepper accordingly. Serve hot.

Feeds six.

Venetian bean soup

A rich and rustic *pasta e fasoi* from the Veneto region of Italy that combines pasta and beans to form a lush, velvety texture that is the soul of good country cooking. Don't forget the benediction: a final swirl of extra virgin olive oil at the end for extra richness.

1½ cups dried borlotti beans
3 tbsp olive oil
1 onion, finely chopped
1 garlic clove, crushed
8 cups chicken broth or water, boiling
salt and freshly ground black pepper
4 canned roma tomatoes, chopped
1 cup of broken tagliatelle or small soup pasta
extra virgin olive oil
2 tbsp grated Parmigiano

Soak beans overnight in cold water.

Heat olive oil in a large pot, add onion and garlic and cook until soft. Add drained beans and boiling broth or water, cover and cook gently for one hour. Add tomatoes and simmer, covered, for another hour.

Remove about half the beans and mash them, then return the paste to the soup, along with the pasta. Cook for 10 or 15 minutes until pasta is tender. Add a swirl of extra virgin olive oil, scatter with grated cheese and serve.

Feeds four.

Zuppa alla Pavese

A humble soup, born of the fear of the good hostess that there isn't enough for her guests. In the course of his battles with the Holy Roman Empire, Francis I, King of France, was sheltered in a local farmhouse. The woman of the house had nothing but stale bread, broth and freshly laid eggs, so she combined them in a soup of spectacular modesty which has been winning hearts ever since. Francis lost the battle, and was captured in 1525, but we won the recipe.

4 free range eggs
4 thick slices of tough country bread
2 tbsp butter
1 litre (1¾ pints) great chicken broth
sea salt and freshly ground pepper
grated Parmigiano for serving

Heat oven to 200°C (400°F). Heat broth to a rolling boil.

Butter the bread on both sides and fry on one side in a hot pan until lightly golden. Cut an egg-sized hole in the middle of each slice, and turn over. Break an egg into each hole and cook, covered, for 3 minutes or so, until egg is cooked and set, but still runny in centre.

Taste broth for salt and pepper.

Arrange the toast in warmed soup bowls. Ladle hot broth around toast and serve immediately, with a bowl of grated Parmigiano.

Feeds four.

Won ton soup

Won means cloud and *ton* means swallow, and together they add up to one of the most popular traditional soups in China. Serve as a whole meal, with as many won tons as you like. This amount of stuffing will make forty, far too many even if you like won tons as much as I do, but it's hard to work with a smaller quantity, so freeze any remaining mixture for next time.

250 g (9 oz) raw prawns
4 dried shiitake mushrooms, soaked
2 green (spring) onion stems, finely chopped
½ tsp salt
½ tsp ground black pepper
250 g (9 oz) minced pork
8 water chestnuts, finely chopped
1 tbsp soy sauce
1 small egg, lightly beaten
1 packet fresh won ton wrappers
1.5 litres (3 pints) good chicken broth
2 slices ginger, peeled
1 Chinese cabbage

Devein and peel prawns, and finely chop. Drain mushrooms, remove stalks, and finely chop. Chop green onion stems.

Mix prawns, mushrooms, green onions, salt, pepper, pork, water chestnuts, soy and egg. Mush the mixture with your hands until it is an icky paste.

Lay won ton skins on work bench. Place one teaspoon of filling in centre of each skin. Brush corners with a little water to help them seal. Fold in half diagonally, so that two corners meet, and press to seal. Brush the two ends with water and twist them up to join and seal.

Cook won tons in a pot of boiling water until they rise to the top. Distribute won tons among soup bowls.

Heat broth and ginger to a high simmer. Cut off any thick stalks of cabbage, and cook the leaves quickly in stock until wilted. Discard ginger and divide stock and cabbage leaves between bowls and serve.

Feeds eight.

P.S. Add 200 g (7 oz) of cooked egg noodles for noodle lovers.

Salad

Salad is a pathway to understanding.

Salads are about patience, faith, compassion, generosity, and wisdom.

In a good salad, there are no passengers.

Every ingredient is there for a reason, and would be missed if it were not present.

The dressing is the final touch, the thing that binds and links everything together, and must be made at the last moment.

It has to be cruel to be kind, in the right measure. The vinegar has to be sharp, so that the olive oil can soothe.

You need to pay attention, to sniff, to lick, to dabble and to dribble.

When you toss a salad, give it the full concentration of all your senses.

Toss it with your hands, keeping an eagle eye out for discoloured leaves or grit.

And eat it in your fingers, before it loses its snap and crackle.

Try to include bitter and astringent leaves like sorrel in what you eat, for a better balance. We don't eat enough of them.

And choose your salad greens with an eye for colour, and not just flavour – carefully coordinated, of course.

I'd hate what you eat to clash with what you wear.

For a truly adult salad, use only babies – the very tips of tender oakleaf, curly endive, radicchio, watercress, lamb's lettuce, dandelion greens and rocket.

Add fresh herbs like chervil, sage, tarragon, dill, basil, marjoram, flat-leaf parsley or mint.

Throw in the petals (only) of edible flowers like borage (*Borage officinalis*), marigold (*Calendula officinalis*), heartsease pansy (*Viola tricolor*), nasturtium (*Tropaeoleum*) and fragrant roses (*Rosa*).

Or go beyond leaves. Make a salad of nothing but raw vegetables: broad beans, carrots, zucchini or asparagus.

Make them emphatic and singular: of one fish, one fruit, one salad green, or one cheese.

Salad deserves a time and a place of its own in our meals, rather than being a bowl of green things in the middle of the table that we would get to if we hadn't eaten quite so much of the real stuff.

We should return to the days of the Renaissance, when salads were made of vegetables and served as a first course.

And maintain the charming and sensible French tradition of cleansing the palate after the main course with a well-dressed leafy green salad.

Or perhaps we should just make the best salad we possibly can from what is available, and forget to serve anything else.

Salad

Beetroot carpaccio
Salmon, orange and avocado
Cole slaw
Mieng kum
Panzanella
Egg and bacon salad
Green salad
Tabbouleh
Octopus salad
Chinatown roast duck and jellyfish
Chilled soba with oysters
Thai pork, mint and chilli
Gado gado
Ensalada de tuna

Beetroot carpaccio

I know it's not a real carpaccio, because the real carpaccio is thinly sliced raw beef in a style created by Giuseppe Cipriani in Venice for a contessa whose doctor forbade her to eat cooked meat. But I will do anything to reinvent beetroot as the glamorous, sweet and seductive vegetable that it is.

4 cooked whole beetroot
2 tbsp lemon juice
sea salt and freshly ground pepper
4 tbsp extra virgin olive oil
2 cups baby rocket leaves
1 tbsp snipped chives

Peel beetroot, and slice as finely as humanly possible. Arrange in overlapping circles on four dinner plates, cover with plastic wrap and chill until required.

Make dressing by whisking lemon juice, sea salt, pepper and olive oil. Divide dressing in half and toss rocket leaves in one half then form into little piles in the centre of each plate.

Scatter beetroot with finely snipped chives and drizzle with remaining dressing until well coated.

Feeds four.

Salmon, orange and avocado

Combining the acid of citrus fruit with raw fish is an old idea. Combining it with the buttery richness of fresh, raw salmon spiced with a cumin vinaigrette in a colourful salad is a new idea whose time has come. If you can't cope with raw salmon, sear the fillet, skin-side down, for a few minutes in a hot pan and leave to rest before proceeding with recipe.

500 g (1 lb) fresh salmon fillet
2 avocados
2 oranges
1 purple onion
mixed salad greens
fresh coriander

Vinaigrette
1 tbsp grated orange rind
1 garlic clove, crushed
4 tbsp olive oil
3 tbsp red wine vinegar
sea salt and pepper
1 tsp cumin seeds, dry roasted

Peel skin away from salmon. Run your fingers over flesh to check for any small bones. Slice into thin sashimi-style slices and set aside.

Peel avocados, remove stones, and cut into long slices. Peel oranges with a sharp knife, including pith, and cut into segments, removing as many pips as possible. Peel onion and slice very, very finely into rings. Wash and shake dry salad leaves.

Whisk orange rind, garlic, olive oil, red wine vinegar, salt, pepper and cumin seeds together in a bowl until thickened. Toss leaves in vinaigrette and arrange in large bowl or on separate serving plates. Arrange salmon, avocado, orange and onion on top, and pour over remaining vinaigrette. Tuck in coriander leaves and serve.

Feeds four.

Cole slaw

The original Dutch recipe for *koolsla*, hot simmered cabbage with oil and vinegar, was taken and transformed by American settlers into a chilled salad that soon became the main attraction of every party. In spite of the main ingredient being cabbage, it shouldn't taste of cabbage alone, but more like a dressy, spicy, creamy, refreshing salady thing. Top with a few barbecued prawns, a lobster salad, or grilled salmon for a classy meal.

½ large Savoy cabbage
250 g (9 oz) cherry tomatoes
2 tbsp white wine vinegar
1 tsp sugar
125 ml (4 fl oz) good quality mayonnaise
  (Broths and Sauces, 209)
125 ml (4 fl oz) natural yoghurt
1 tsp ground ginger
1 tsp Dijon mustard
sea salt and freshly ground black pepper

Cut off outer leaves and cut cabbage in half. Slice cabbage as finely as possible, and I mean finely. Cover cabbage with cold water and chill for 1 hour.

Cut tomatoes in half, or quarters, depending on their size. Mix vinegar and sugar until sugar dissolves. Drain cabbage and toss with cherry tomatoes, vinegar and sugar.

Mix mayonnaise, yoghurt, ginger, mustard, salt and pepper in a bowl. Toss vinegared cabbage and tomatoes in dressing with your hands, until well-coated. Taste for seasoning, and adjust vinegar, salt and pepper accordingly. Chill for 2 hours. Give it a quick toss before serving.

Feeds six.

Mieng kum

You look at all these things and think you could never put them in your mouth, raw, just like that. And then you wrap up bits of tangy lime, crunchy coconut, dried shrimps, shallots, chilli and roasted peanuts in a fresh leaf and take a big bite and it all magically melds into one fantastic, power-packed sensation in the true Thai manner. You can find glossy, green pointed betel leaves (Thai: *bai cha plu*) at Asian greengrocers, or use spinach or lettuce leaves instead.

½ cup palm sugar, chopped
1½ cups water
5 tbsp grated coconut
1 tbsp shrimp paste (belacan)
3 shallots, finely sliced
1 tbsp peanuts
1 tbsp dried shrimps
1 tsp sliced galangal or ginger
2 tbsp finely diced shallots
2 tbsp finely diced lime, with skin
2 tbsp finely diced ginger
2 tbsp dried shrimps
2 tbsp roasted peanuts
1 tbsp finely chopped chilli
10 fresh cha plu leaves or small lettuce leaves,
  washed and dried

Bring sugar and water to the boil and stir until sugar has melted. Heat a dry frypan and toast the grated coconut until lightly golden. Remove the coconut and dry-fry the shrimp paste until fragrant.

Pound together or blend shrimp paste, one tablespoon of the coconut, shallots, peanuts, shrimps and galangal or ginger until mushy. Combine the paste with sugar syrup, and simmer, stirring, for 15 minutes or so until it thickens. Cool to room temperature.

Arrange remaining toasted coconut and remaining ingredients – shallots, lime, ginger, dried shrimps, roasted peanuts and chilli – in small piles or small bowls on a serving platter or tray. Add a small bowl of the sauce, and a stack of the leaves.

Take a leaf, put a few assorted tastes on it, top with a spoonful of sauce, wrap and eat.

Makes ten.

Panzanella

'Bread is the foundation of all other foods', wrote sixteenth-century Florentine writer Domenico Romoli. The large round loaves of traditional unsalted Tuscan bread lasted so long, Tuscans soon learnt how to make stale bread taste wonderful. In a marvellous bit of early cross-merchandising, they also made good use of their equally beloved olive oil.

1 stale loaf of good sourdough bread
6 ripe tomatoes
2 garlic cloves, crushed
1 tbsp salted capers, rinsed
4 anchovy fillets, rinsed
sea salt and freshly ground black pepper
6 tbsp extra virgin olive oil
1 tbsp red wine vinegar
2 red peppers (capsicums)
2 tbsp black olives, stoned
a few sprigs of basil

Slice the bread thickly and cut off the crusts. Grill until brown on both sides, then tear into chunky cubes and set aside.

Dunk tomatoes in boiling water for a few seconds, then peel and cut in half. Hold the tomatoes over a strainer over a bowl, squeeze gently to remove juice and seeds. Cut tomatoes into chunks and set aside.

Add garlic, capers and anchovies, salt and pepper to the strained tomato juice and mash well. Add olive oil and red wine vinegar and stir. Pour dressing over bread and leave for one hour.

Grill or roast the peppers until blackened and blistered. Peel off skin, cut in half, deseed, and cut each half into strips. Place some soaked bread on the bottom of a large bowl, and top with some of the tomatoes, the garlic-anchovy paste, pepper strips, olives and torn basil leaves. Add more bread, and a final layer of all ingredients, and leave for an hour at room temperature. Serve with an extra drizzle of extra virgin olive oil.

Feeds four.

Egg and bacon salad

The secret of this salad is the technique the French call *en chiffonnade*, chiffon meaning rags. Take a few leaves at a time and roll them into a tight cigar before finely cutting. The leaves unroll into tiny, delicate 'rags'. It's quite boring having to turn an entire bunch of spinach into little rags, but the unreal lightness of the salad is well worth the effort.

2 free range eggs
4 thin rashers rindless bacon
1 big bunch of spinach
1½ tbsp red wine vinegar
sea salt and freshly ground black pepper
4 tbsp extra virgin olive oil

Cook the eggs in simmering salted water for 8 minutes, cool, and peel. Put each egg through an egg-slicer lengthwise, then turn at right angles and put it through again. Otherwise, finely chop by hand into tiny, tiny dice.

Cut bacon into tiny dice. Fry bacon in a non-stick frypan until crisp and golden, and drain off the fat.

Trim stems from spinach and wash leaves well in a sink of cold water. Drain and pat dry with paper towel. Place the largest leaf on the chopping board and make a pile of 6 or so large leaves on top of it. Roll up the leaves lengthwise, like a cigarette, and cut into thin strips about .5 cm (¼ in) wide. Continue with remaining leaves, until they are all finely sliced.

Make the dressing by combining vinegar, salt and pepper in a large bowl. Slowly whisk in olive oil until the mixture thickens. Toss spinach in the dressing and pile high on a large dinner plate or serving platter. Scatter with finely chopped egg, and finely chopped bacon.

Feeds two as an entrée, or four as a salad on the side.

Green salad

A green salad does not, and has never had, cherry tomatoes and bean shoots in it. It has only the delicate, tiny tips of herbs and leaves. That's why it is called a green salad. Otherwise it would be called a green, red, yellow, pink and white salad. A French housewife's trick: throw in a spoonful of the cooking juices from a roasted chicken or lamb to the green leaf salad you will be serving with or after the roast.

around 2 cups of the tips of mixed cresses and leaves:
  oakleaf, curly endive, radicchio, watercress,
  lamb's lettuce, dandelion greens, rocket
around ½ cup of the tips of mixed fresh herbs:
  chervil, sage, tarragon, dill, basil, marjoram, mint
2 tbsp red wine vinegar or lemon juice
1 tsp finely grated lemon rind
sea salt and freshly ground black pepper
4 tbsp extra virgin olive oil

Wash leaves carefully, and dry them even more carefully. Whisk red wine vinegar or lemon juice with lemon rind, sea salt and pepper. Add olive oil slowly, while whisking, until dressing thickens. Toss the leaves gently in the dressing, using your hands. Pile leaves high on a plate.

P.S. The Romans often added edible flowers to their table. Try mixing the petals of fresh marigolds, daisies, pansies, roses and chive flowers and tossing them through the salad.

Feeds four as a salad, or one salad freak as a meal.

Tabbouleh

That great – and greatly abused – Middle Eastern herb salad, tabbouleh, is traditionally served with small, tender vine leaves, so that you can scoop it up and eat it in big, juicy mouthfuls. It should be so lemony that just the thought of it makes your mouth water. I don't use garlic, preferring the freshness of green (spring) onions instead. Make it as close to the time of eating as possible.

½ cup bulghur (cracked wheat)
½ cup cold water
4 green (spring) onions
1 small cucumber
2 tomatoes
3 bunches flat-leaf parsley
2 bunches mint
3 tbsp extra virgin olive oil
3 tbsp lemon juice
½ tsp ground cumin
1 tsp sea salt

Soak bulghur in water for 20 minutes. Drain and squeeze dry. Chop green onions finely.

Peel cucumber, cut in half and scoop out seeds. Chop cucumber finely. Dunk tomatoes in a pot of boiling water for 10 seconds and peel. Cut tomatoes in half and squeeze out seeds. Cut remaining flesh into small dice. Wash parsley and mint and dry thoroughly. Chop parsley and mint leaves finely. Toss bulghur with parsley and mint. Add green onions, cucumber and tomato and toss well.

Mix olive oil, lemon juice, cumin and sea salt and pour over salad. Taste for sharpness and add more lemon juice if need be. Toss well and serve with vine leaves or lettuce leaves for scooping.

Feeds four.

Octopus salad

A refreshing tapa of baby octopus made famous by the cosy little Bar Pulpito in Madrid's magnificent Plaza de Mayor. If you don't over-cook the octopus to hell, the effect is the same as at Bar Pulpito.

500 g (1 lb) baby octopus
1 tomato, finely chopped
½ red pepper (capsicum), finely chopped
½ onion, finely chopped
¼ cup fruity olive oil
2 tbsp white wine vinegar
3 tbsp water
salt and freshly ground pepper

Cut the head off each octopus, just below the eyes, and discard. Cut each octopus in half and discard the hard little beak inside. Clean well and pat dry.

Bring a large pot of water to the boil and cook octopus for 1 minute. Drain well. Mix octopus, tomato, red pepper and onion.

Whisk together olive oil, vinegar, water, salt and pepper in a small bowl and pour over octopus. Refrigerate overnight before serving with crusty bread and a cold beer.

Feeds four.

Chinatown roast duck and jellyfish

Don't be scared by the fact that dried jellyfish looks an awful lot like a plastic shower curtain as you unwrap it from its packet. Once soaked, the salted and sun-dried skin comes up like chamois, with a slight crunch and subtle sea flavour that combines happily with rich and succulent roast duck from Chinatown. Serve at room temperature as a summer salad.

500 g (1 lb) dried jellyfish, from Asian foodstores
1 cucumber, peeled
2 carrots, peeled
4 sticks celery
1 Chinese roasted duck or chicken
2 tbsp sesame oil
2 tbsp soy sauce
2 tbsp vinegar
1 tsp sugar

Soak the jellyfish in a large pot of water for 24 hours, changing the water 3 times. Trim each piece neatly, and roll tightly, like a sponge roll. Cut across roll into thin strips 1 cm (½ in) wide. Cover strips with warm water and soak for 20 minutes, then drain and cool. Pat dry with paper towel.

Cut cucumber lengthwise, and scoop out seeds. Cut carrots, cucumber and celery into very thin matchsticks.

Remove all flesh and skin from duck, discarding bones and excess fat, and cut into very fine slivers. Combine with jellyfish and vegetables. Mix sesame oil, soy sauce, vinegar and sugar in a bowl, and gently toss through salad.

Feeds six.

Chilled soba with oysters

Traditionally, soba (buckwheat) noodles are served chilled, with a simple dipping sauce of soy, mirin and dashi. On a hot day, they are more cooling than an air conditioner and a swimming pool combined. I have added chilled, fresh oysters for a touch of untraditional luxury, thereby probably blowing the zen of the dish out of the water, but it's worth it.

2 cups water
5 g (1/8 oz) instant dashi powder
1 tbsp mirin (sweet rice wine)
1 tbsp soy sauce
400 g (14 oz) dried soba noodles
2 tsp dried wakame seaweed
2 green (spring) onion greens
1 small cucumber
1 tsp sesame oil
12 freshly opened oysters, chilled
2 tbsp Japanese pickled ginger

To make dressing, bring water to the boil, and add dashi powder, mirin and soy, stirring. Remove from heat and allow to cool. Adjust seasoning to taste.

Cook noodles in plenty of boiling water for 6 to 8 minutes until al dente, tender but still firm to the bite. Drain and rinse in cold water, then drain again.

Soak wakame in a small bowl of warm water for 15 minutes, where it will expand like crazy. Drain and set aside.

Finely cut onion greens on the diagonal and set aside. Peel cucumber, cut in half lengthwise and scoop out seeds. Cut into thin slices, then again into matchstick lengths.

Toss cucumber, noodles, drained wakame and sesame oil together in a bowl, and distribute among four Japanese bowls. Moisten each bowl with a spoonful or two of the dressing. Top with chilled oysters, 3 per bowl, moisten with a little remaining dressing, and scatter with onion greens.

Serve with Japanese pickled ginger.

Feeds four.

Thai pork, mint and chilli

A refreshing Thai salad that combines the typical tastes of Thailand, being hot, sour, sweet and salty all at the same time. Just for fun, serve it on a thick slice of fresh pineapple, which can then be eaten as well.

400 g (14 oz) pork fillet
2 lemon grass stalks
2 garlic cloves
2 coriander roots
2 small red chillies, seeded
1 tbsp peanut oil
4 tbsp Thai fish sauce (nam pla)
4 tbsp lime juice
2 tsp sugar
4 shallots, peeled and sliced
1 tsp rice, roasted and ground
1 cup fresh mint leaves
1 cup fresh coriander leaves
2 tbsp deep-fried shallots, from Asian food store
1 fresh, ripe pineapple

Cut pork fillet into 2 lengths. Peel lemon grass and cut the tender white stem into very fine slices. Pound garlic, coriander roots, lemon grass and chilli into a rough paste. Rub pork with paste and leave for at least 2 hours.

Heat grill, and rub pork with peanut oil, rubbing off most of the marinade. Grill pork on all sides, until tender and cooked through. Leave to rest for 10 minutes, then slice finely and reassemble into original shape.

Mix fish sauce, lime juice, sugar, sliced shallots, roasted rice powder, mint leaves and coriander leaves and lightly toss.

Cut a whole pineapple lengthwise, either side of centre, into a 2 cm (3/4 in) 'plate', including leaves. Arrange pork on top of the pineapple slice on a large serving platter, and pour dressing on top. Scatter deep-fried shallots on top and serve.

Feeds four, as part of a Thai meal with rice.

Gado gado

For years, gado gado has been the vegetarian's punishment, a heavy, bland beancurd and vegetable salad doused in peanut sauce. But when it's fresh, lively, crisp, crunchy and highly spicy, it immediately becomes the vegetarian's – and everyone else's – reward.

3 squares fresh beancurd
1 cos (romaine) lettuce
1 cucumber
1 carrot, peeled
2 tbsp plain flour
2 tbsp vegetable oil
1 cup bean shoots
1 cup cabbage, roughly chopped
1 cup cauliflower, broken into florets
1 cup green beans
1/2 bunch spinach, roughly chopped
1 tomato, sliced
1 hard-boiled egg, peeled
1 potato, cooked
1 cup peanut sauce (Broths and Sauces, 209)
1 tbsp deep-fried shallots

Place beancurd squares on a dinner plate and weight with a second plate on top for one hour. Drain off water and pat dry. Separate leaves from lettuce, wash, dry and shred finely. Peel cucumber and slice finely. Cut the carrot into thin matchsticks.

Cut beancurd into strips, dredge in flour and fry quickly in hot oil. Drain and pat dry.

Pour boiling water over bean shoots, drain and rinse. Steam cabbage, cauliflower, carrot and green beans until lightly cooked. Lightly steam spinach until wilted. Cool to room temperature.

Arrange cucumber in an overlapping circle on the base of each of 4 dinner plates, as the base of a pyramid. Arrange sliced tomato on top, and then shredded lettuce. Top with a sprinkling of bean shoots, then the cabbage, spinach, cauliflower, carrot and green beans. Cut egg and potato into small cubes. Add beancurd, egg and potato on top of pyramids. Pour peanut sauce over the top, and sprinkle with deep-fried shallots.

Feeds four.

Ensalada de tuna

Both avocado and the serrano chilli (bright dark green, around four centimetres or two inches long, with a clean, hot bite) were indigenous to Mexico long before the Spaniards arrived, giving them plenty of time to come up with a refreshing salsa such as this. I added the tuna because it seemed to deserve it, and because I had some fresh tuna.

1 large avocado
1/4 cup fresh lime juice
1 yellow pepper
2 roma tomatoes
2 tbsp finely diced red onion
1 serrano chilli, finely chopped, with seeds
2 tsp finely chopped fresh coriander
sea salt
100 g (3 1/2 oz) fresh sashimi-quality tuna per person

Peel avocado, remove stone, and chop finely into tiny dice. Combine avocado and lime juice and set aside. Cut yellow pepper and tomatoes into tiny dice, discarding seeds.

Mix avocado with diced tomato, yellow pepper, red onion, serrano chilli, coriander and salt and chill for 30 minutes.

Slice tuna, then cut into small cubes. Toss tuna very lightly through the salsa. Spoon salsa into cocktail glasses or drain lightly and serve on a few corn husks.

Serve with corn chips for dipping or scooping.

Feeds four.

Eating outdoors makes us anxious. We take too much.
We want to take civilisation with us into the wilderness, thereby destroying both the idea of a picnic,
and the idea of wilderness.
You really only need bread, fresh fruit, something cool and provocative to drink, and one other thing.
It could be a huge sweet onion tart, warm from the oven, an enormous terrine spiked with herbs and nuts,
or a pile of freshly cooked prawns in their shells, but it will be the best food you have ever eaten.
When in doubt, make sandwiches, the ultimate portable food of the people,
filled with finely sliced ham off the bone, or bagels stuffed with smoked salmon and egg mayo.
Don't take butter, which melts into yellow grease; take a small bottle of extra virgin olive oil instead, for bread and salads.
Any more than that, and you spoil a picnic faster than bad weather and ants.
A loaf of bread, a jug of wine, remember?
After all, the most important ingredients are already present:
fresh air,
a sense of space,
of letting go,
of winding down,
of blissing out,
of sunshine on your shoulders,
and twigs under foot, of bird song and distant barking dogs, and delicate little flowers you admire in passing,
and the tracks of nocturnal animals by the side of the river, and carpets of green grass in city parks or white sand on beaches,
and eating without a table, in your hands, and finding your appetite again, for food, and life, and friends,
and good books and lying on your back
and staring at the clouds and speaking only when you feel like it and letting cold wine trickle down your throat
and squeezing left over lemons on your hands to clean them,
and going to sleep in the open air for an hour after lunch,
and not having any dishes worth speaking of,
and getting home tired and grumpy but completely, utterly pleased with yourself.

Country terrine

Melt 1 tbsp butter or olive oil in frypan, and cook 2 finely chopped onions until soft, then set aside to cool.
Chop one slice of rindless bacon, and mix with 200 g (7 oz) pork mince, 200 g (7 oz) veal mince
and 200 g (7 oz) chicken mince.
Remove crusts from 4 thick slices of stale bread, and crumb in a food processor.
Add crumbs to the meat with cooked onion, 3 slices of ham (chopped), 2 tbsp pistachio nuts, 10 juniper berries,
1 tbsp fresh thyme, 1 bay leaf, good pinches of ground mace and nutmeg, 1 tsp salt, 1/2 tsp pepper and 2 tbsp brandy.
Mix well with your hands, and leave to stand in a cool place for a couple of hours.
Heat oven to 180°C (350°F). Line an earthenware terrine or loaf tin with 10 or so slices of thin rindless bacon,
keeping 2 in reserve.
Prepare a water bath by half-filling a roasting pan with water.
Work 2 eggs into the meat mixture with your hands, then tip everything into the terrine, top with the last of the bacon,
and cover top with foil, tied with string.
Place terrine in water bath and cook at 180°C (350°F) for around an hour and a half, or until the terrine has shrunk
from the sides of the tin.
Leave to cool completely, then place on tray and store in fridge overnight.
The juices will set into a kind of aspic around the terrine, which you can leave on, or trim.
Leave terrine in the tin for travelling, and turn out when ready to eat.
Feeds eight.

Give yourself time to stew.

Now that we have a stir-fry down to ten minutes and a barbecue to twelve minutes, it's time we cooked something with time as a major ingredient.

Slow food like a good stew doesn't have to take up any more of your time than fast food, because it cooks itself.

Let the stove do the work. That's what it's there for.

Stews use time as a friend, not an enemy.

Set a soupy pot of meat and vegetables to bubble and braise on Saturday afternoon while you go and do something else.

Or make a stew on Sunday morning to have during the week.

Soak dried beans when you get up in the morning, and they will be ready to cook when you get home at night. Don't rush it.

You want a good, laid-back stew full of relaxed meats and vegetables.

A good stew will barely break the surface with little more than a burp and a hiccup.

Get it to the right temperature and leave it, without massive swings to high and low.

Nobody ever speaks of stews as being healthy, but slow cooking with vegetables and stock brings out heaps of flavour without the need for additional fats.

Besides, you have time to skim off the fat to your heart's content.

Or cool the cooked stew and let the fat rise to the surface overnight, and scrape it off the next day.

To start, you need a nice big pot with a close-fitting lid, lots of onions, carrots, and celery, good wine and broth.

Toss in a bouquet garni of parsley and thyme sprigs and bay leaf wrapped in a sheath of leek skin and tied with string (and don't forget to fish it out later).

Then leave it alone.

Stews don't want you to hover.

They don't like fuss.

In fact, they don't even want you in the kitchen.

All they need is help to get started.

Stews

Braised lamb shanks
Chicken waterzooï
Roman chicken and tomatoes
Ratatouille
Beef rendang
Tripes à la Niçoise
Osso buco
Lancashire hotpot
Lamb navarin
Hungarian gulyas
Chicken and thyme stew
Chili con carne

Braised lamb shanks

Traditionally poor people's food, this is the new luxury – food cooked with no rushing, no pressure, and no worries. And the leftovers make a sensational *sugo* for pasta for tomorrow night. If there are any leftovers.

2 carrots
2 parsnips
2 onions
2 leeks
3 tbsp olive oil
6 lamb shanks
2 celery stalks, finely chopped
2 garlic cloves, crushed
200 ml (7 fl oz) white wine
400 g (14 oz) canned tomatoes
10 sprigs of fresh thyme
4 sprigs of parsley
4 sprigs of rosemary
1 bay leaf
200 to 400 ml (7 to 14 fl oz) water or broth
sea salt and freshly ground black pepper

Peel carrots, parsnips and onions and finely chop. Chop leeks in half lengthwise, and cut into 5 cm (2 in) lengths.

Heat olive oil in a heavy-bottomed lidded casserole that will take direct heat, and brown lamb shanks really well (until dark brown) on top of the stove. Remove shanks, add carrot, parsnip, onion, leeks, celery and garlic, and cook for 10 minutes until they start to soften. Add white wine and scrape up any residue attached to bottom of pan. Return shanks to pan, packing them in tightly.

Add tomatoes, thyme, parsley, rosemary, bay leaf, and water or broth. Bring to the boil, then reduce heat to a very gentle simmer, cover, and cook for 2 hours, skimming occasionally. Add extra liquid if need be, but the idea of braising is for the meat to be cooked in its own juices.

Remove shanks from pot and keep hot. Strain the sauce through a fine sieve into a clean pan, pressing down to extract all liquid. Boil sauce, stirring, until reduced to a thickened sauce. Taste for salt and pepper and adjust accordingly.

Serve one shank per normal person and pour the sauce on top, or remove meat from the bones and return it to the sauce before serving. Serve on a bed of parsley mash (Potatoes, 116) or creamy polenta.

Feeds four to six.

Chicken waterzooï

Waterzooï (pronounced something like varterzoy) simply means to simmer in water. It's an old Flemish dish that can be made of freshwater fish and eel but I love the creamy chicken version from Ghent in Belgium, a one-pot wonder of times past. Serve with a bowl of small boiled potatoes rolled in butter and parsley.

1.6 kg (3 lb) free range chicken
3 medium leeks, cleaned and trimmed
4 medium carrots, peeled
2 celery stalks
2 bay leaves
1/4 tsp salt
1/2 tsp black peppercorns
3 egg yolks
125 ml (4 fl oz) thick cream
sea salt and freshly ground black pepper
2 tbsp finely chopped parsley, or sprigs of parsley

Wash and dry chicken. Place chicken in a large pot, and add enough cold water to just cover. Bring to the boil, skimming off any froth that rises to the surface. Slice leeks finely, and slice carrots and celery into 1 cm (1/2 in) slices. Add leeks, carrots, celery, bay leaves, salt and peppercorns, and simmer with a slight bubble for around 40 minutes, until chicken is tender and carrots are cooked.

Strain 2 cups of the broth into a smaller saucepan, and bring to the boil. Boil until broth is reduced to around 1 cup. Beat egg yolks and cream together in a bowl. Add a ladleful of hot broth, beating, then continue to beat as you add remaining broth. Return sauce to saucepan and heat very gently, stirring well, until sauce thickens slightly. Taste for seasoning, and keep sauce warm.

Remove chicken from broth and cut it into eight pieces – 2 drumsticks, 2 thighs and each breast into 2. Strain the vegetables from remaining broth, and arrange on the base of a large, warm serving platter, or in 4 warm soup or pasta plates. Arrange 1 or 2 joints of chicken on top of vegetables.

Pour the cream sauce over the chicken, scatter with parsley and serve.

P.S. For a pretty vegetable garnish, cut a portion of leek, carrot and celery into fine matchsticks, and set aside. When ready to serve, dunk them in a sieve into the hot broth for one minute, then drain. Scatter on top of the dishes when serving, with the parsley.

Feeds four.

Roman chicken and tomatoes

The flavours in this screamingly simple stew – chicken, garlic, red pepper, tomato and ham – are so in tune with each other, that they fuse into a whole almost without you doing anything. We like that in a dish. Serve on a bed of fine tagliatelle tossed in butter and chopped parsley.

2 tbsp olive oil
4 chicken drumsticks
4 chicken thighs
2 garlic cloves, squashed
2 slices of ham or bacon, 1 cm (½ in) thick
100 ml (3½ fl oz) dry white wine
4 medium tomatoes, finely chopped
2 red peppers (capsicums), cut into strips
sea salt and freshly ground black pepper
1 tbsp finely chopped parsley

Heat olive oil in a heavy-bottomed frypan and add chicken pieces. Brown well on both sides, leaving them on the first side without moving them for over 5 minutes before turning. Drain off excess fat as it renders from the chicken.

Add garlic and ham or bacon and cook for 5 minutes. Add white wine and allow to bubble and evaporate. Add tomatoes and red peppers, cover and cook for 10 minutes. Check the amount of liquid in pan, and add half a cup of hot water if dry.

Add salt and pepper, cover and cook gently for 20 to 30 minutes until chicken is tender. Stir in parsley and serve.

Feeds four.

Ratatouille

'Rat-a-tooey' it has always been, but 'rat-a-twee' it should be. What we've done to the language, we've also done to this Provençal vegetable stew, which requires a bit more care in the cooking than it usually gets. In summer, grill the vegetables and sandwich them together with stewed onion and tomato, as shown here. In winter, just stew it all together. *Ratatouille* means to toss together, so don't worry if it looks a right mess.

2 eggplants (aubergines)
3 onions
6 tomatoes
2 garlic cloves
4 tbsp olive oil
1 bay leaf
4 sprigs rosemary
10 basil leaves
2 red peppers (capsicums)
3 zucchini
sea salt and freshly ground black pepper

Slice eggplants lengthwise, sprinkle with salt, and leave for one hour to draw out any bitter juices. Rinse well and pat dry.

Slice onions into rings. Cut tomatoes in half and squeeze out and discard seeds and juices. Cut flesh into chunks. Peel garlic cloves and squash flat.

Heat olive oil in frypan and cook onions and garlic for 10 minutes until soft. Add tomatoes, bay leaf, rosemary sprigs and basil leaves, pepper and salt, and cook for 10 to 15 minutes, raising the heat to evaporate any excess juices. Remove from heat and allow to cool slightly.

Cut each red pepper lengthwise into four, discarding seeds. Cut each zucchini lengthwise into fine slices, discarding the outer slices.

Brush eggplant, red pepper and zucchini with olive oil and grill until cooked and well marked. Layer eggplant and red pepper, then tomato stew, more red pepper, eggplant and zucchini, finishing with a dollop of tomato stew.

Serve hot, warm or cold.

Feeds four.

Beef rendang

Serve this big pot of aromatic Malaysian *rendang daging* with steamed rice and roti bread, warmed in the oven or in a hot pan; or even the famous Malaysian lacy pancakes, *roti jala* (Pantry, 219). The sauce, even though it is only of coating consistency, is so rich, you really need to treat it as an exotic condiment rather than an excuse to eat beef.

600 g (1¼ lb) topside beef
3 tbsp desiccated coconut
2 garlic cloves
6 shallots or 1 onion, sliced
2 peeled stalks of lemon grass, sliced
6 dried chillies, soaked and drained
2 tbsp freshly grated ginger
1 tsp turmeric powder
1 tsp salt
1 tsp sugar
2 tbsp vegetable oil
1 cup thick coconut milk
½ cup water
1 tsp tamarind dissolved in 1 tbsp water
4 star anise
1 cinnamon stick

Cut beef into bite-sized cubes and set aside.

Heat a dry frypan, add coconut and toast until lightly golden. Pound or blend together the toasted coconut, garlic, shallots or onion, lemon grass, drained chillies, ginger, turmeric, salt and sugar until you have a paste.

Heat oil in a heavy-bottomed frypan. Add paste and cook for 5 minutes, stirring, until fragrant. Add beef and stir-fry for 5 minutes, until it changes colour. Add coconut milk, water, tamarind water, star anise and cinnamon stick and bring to the boil, stirring constantly. Simmer over gentle heat, uncovered, for 1½ hours, until the sauce has almost cooked away, and the beef is dark and tender. Add a little water if it dries out, but the sauce should really only coat the meat.

Feeds four to six.

Tripes à la Niçoise

Tripe prepared in the style of Nice, with tomatoes and garlic is an aromatic, full-flavoured meal that could just turn more people on to appreciating the inner story. Either prepare your own tripe (Pantry, 218) or look for firm, perky, lightly bleached tripe at a good butcher.

3 tbsp olive oil
1 kg (2 lb) onions, sliced
2 garlic cloves, crushed
3 carrots, peeled and finely chopped
1 kg (2 lb) bleached, prepared honeycomb tripe
400 g (14 oz) canned tomatoes with juices
 or 4 tomatoes, peeled, seeded and chopped
1 wine glass dry white wine
2 bay leaves
1 tbsp finely chopped parsley
1 tbsp fresh thyme leaves
sea salt and freshly ground black pepper
up to 500 ml (18 fl oz) veal, chicken broth or water

Heat olive oil in a large, heavy-bottomed, lidded, heat-proof casserole, and cook onions, garlic and carrots on top of the stove for 20 minutes until soft. Heat oven to 160°C (325°F).

Rinse tripe well, drain and pat dry. Cut into strips the length of your little finger, around 1 cm (½ in) wide. Add tripe and cook for 10 minutes, tossing well. Add tomatoes, wine, bay leaves, parsley, thyme, salt and pepper. Pour in just enough broth to cover the lot, and bring to the boil. Reduce to a simmer, cover with a sheet of foil and tightly close the casserole lid.

Place in centre of oven to cook for 1½ to 2 hours, depending on your tripe, until it is tender but not overly soft. Return casserole to the top of the stove and bring to a high simmer before serving, reducing any excess liquid – the tripe should be coated in the juices, rather than swimming in them. Taste for seasoning and adjust accordingly.

Serve in warmed, shallow pasta plates, with a side bowl of boiled new potatoes tossed in butter and parsley.

Feeds four.

Osso buco

Osso buco means 'bone with a hole' in Italian. The bone is veal shank, and the hole is filled with rich bone marrow. If you're a marrow lover, cook this in a wide, shallow casserole so that you can stand the bones upright and not lose the jelly inside. I swear I only cook this so I can sprinkle the traditional lemony, garlicky gremolata on top, which is a bit like ordering fish and chips because you like salt. (Make gremolata for all sorts of dishes, not just osso buco: it's fantastic sprinkled over and into mashed potato.)

4 slices of veal shank, 5 cm (2 in) thick
 with marrow bone in centre, or 10 small pieces
seasoned flour
2 tbsp butter
1 tbsp olive oil
1 onion, peeled and chopped
2 celery stalks, chopped
1 carrot, peeled and chopped
1 garlic clove, crushed
1 cup dry white wine
1 cup canned tomatoes, chopped
2 tbsp tomato paste (concentrate)
1 cup veal or chicken broth

Gremolata
2 garlic cloves, crushed
½ cup finely chopped flat-leaf parsley
grated rind of half a lemon

Coat the veal lightly with the flour. Melt butter and oil and fry veal until browned all over. Remove veal and cook onion, celery, carrot and garlic until onion is soft and translucent, adding a little extra olive oil if necessary.

Return veal to the pan, then add wine and bring to the boil. Allow to bubble until the liquid is reduced to about one-third the original volume. Add tomatoes, tomato paste and veal or chicken broth, then cover and simmer for 1½ hours.

Mix together the garlic, parsley and lemon rind to make a gremolata. Serve osso buco, with plenty of sauce, in pasta bowls, or on dinner plates with mashed potato, soft polenta, or saffron-flavoured risotto. Sprinkle the gremolata on top, and serve hot.

Feeds four.

Lancashire hotpot

The original one-pot-wonder, Lancashire hotpot is made of lambs' neck and kidneys layered with potatoes and onions and not much else. I've added the sweet flavours of carrot, celery, herbs, smoky ham and white wine. I don't add the kidneys, but I include them here for purist Lancastrians.

8 lamb neck chops
3 lamb's kidneys
2 carrots
2 celery stalks
2 onions
2 tbsp butter
1 tbsp olive oil
1 thick slice speck (smoked ham)
½ cup white wine
750 ml (26 fl oz) water or chicken broth, heated
2 bay leaves
6 potatoes, peeled
3 small sprigs rosemary
1 tbsp butter

Cut excess fat from lamb neck chops. Skin kidneys, and slice the meat on either side of the centre gristly bits. Set aside.

Peel carrots and chop into small dice. Slice celery finely, and chop onions finely. Heat butter and oil in a heavy-based frypan, add carrots, celery, onion, and the slice of speck, and cook for 10 minutes until they start to soften. Add white wine and allow to bubble and reduce until almost gone. Add hot water or broth, and bay leaves. Heat oven to 180°C (350°F).

Slice the potatoes into 1 cm (½ in) discs, and arrange a layer of potatoes on the base of a heavy, lidded casserole. Arrange lamb neck chops and kidneys on top and tuck in little sprigs of rosemary. Spoon over the broth and vegetables, and press down lightly. Finish with a layer of sliced potatoes on top. Scatter with little dobs of butter, cover, and bring to the boil on top of the stove. When simmering, transfer to oven and bake for 2 to 3 hours until the top potatoes are golden brown, but the meat is still juicy.

Serve to each person a deep spoonful of 1 or 2 lamb neck chops and kidneys with the crusty potato topping, and spoon juices around it.

Feeds four.

Lamb navarin

Traditionally cooked in Paris and its surrounding countryside to herald the arrival of spring, a navarin of lamb is a good old-fashioned stew, made with plenty of onions, carrots and parsnips. Serve with creamy mash and fresh herbs.

3 tbsp light olive oil
1 kg to 1.5 kg (2 lb to 3 lb) lamb shoulder or leg,
  boned and cut into cubes
1 tbsp plain flour
2 tbsp light olive oil
2 cloves garlic, crushed
1 onion, finely chopped
2 celery stalks, finely chopped
8 small pickling onions
4 carrots, peeled and cut into short lengths
2 parsnips, peeled and cut into short lengths
8 small potatoes, peeled
400 g (14 oz) tomatoes
  or 4 tomatoes, peeled and seeded
sprigs of thyme
2 tbsp finely chopped parsley
1 bay leaf
salt and pepper
2 cups chicken broth or water
200 g (7 oz) green beans, blanched

Heat oven to 180°C (350°F). Heat a little of the olive oil in a heavy-bottomed casserole dish that will take direct heat, and brown one-third of the meat. Remove meat, add a little more olive oil, and continue process until all meat is browned. Sprinkle the last lot of meat with flour, salt and pepper, and cook for 2 or 3 minutes on both sides until flour also browns. Add remaining meat and mix well.

Remove meat, and add remaining 2 tablespoons of oil. Add garlic and chopped onion and cook until soft. Add celery, pickling onions and carrots and cook for 5 minutes. Return meat to pan, then add parsnips, potatoes, tomatoes, thyme, parsley, bay leaf and salt and pepper and chicken broth or liquid to come two-thirds of the way up the side of the casserole. Bring to the boil on top of stove then place in oven for 1½ hours. Remove once or twice during that time and turn meat and vegetables over so that they cook evenly. Toss blanched green beans into the casserole for the last 5 minutes of cooking, and serve.

Feeds four to six.

Hungarian gulyas

Hungarian restaurateur and author George Lang says that what is usually served in the name of Hungarian goulasch (gulyas) shouldn't happen to a Rumanian. (My apologies to all Rumanians who feel offended by this). The real thing, which was originally a shepherd's way of preserving beef for the long sojourns out with the flock, should be beefy, hot and quite soupy. Serve with bread or with home-made noodles.

2 tbsp olive oil
2 onions, roughly chopped
1 garlic clove, crushed
1 kg (2 lb) beef (blade), cut into 2 cm (¾ in) cubes
pinch of caraway seeds
salt
1 tbsp sweet paprika
1 litre (1 quart) water or beef broth, boiling
350 g (12 oz) canned or fresh tomatoes, chopped
1 green pepper (capsicum), cut into rings
4 medium potatoes, peeled and finely diced
1 tbsp finely chopped marjoram

Heat olive oil and cook onions and garlic for 10 minutes until soft. Add the beef and cook, stirring, for 10 minutes, until browned. Remove from heat and add caraway seeds, salt and paprika, stirring. Return to heat and add boiling water or broth, stirring well.

Cook gently for 1 hour, partly covered, skimming occasionally. Add tomatoes, green pepper and potatoes, and cook for another hour until meat and vegetables are tender and the juices are still a bit soupy. Give the whole dish a big strong stir towards the end to help the cooked potatoes dissolve and thicken the sauce.

Taste for salt and pepper and serve in wide shallow soup or pasta bowls with a ladleful or two of sauce. Scatter marjoram on top and serve hot.

Feeds six.

Chicken and thyme stew

A simple stew in the French country style with the sweetness of leeks and the floral qualities of thyme. Serve with a fresh green mixed-leaf salad, finish with a little fresh goat's cheese, and you are eating like that middle-class dream, a peasant.

5 chicken drumsticks
5 chicken thighs
enough flour to coat chicken
1 tbsp light olive oil
1 tbsp butter
3 leeks, trimmed, washed and sliced
2 carrots, finely chopped
4 celery stalks, finely chopped
½ cup white wine
1 cup chicken broth or water
300 g (11 oz) canned tomatoes
4 potatoes, peeled and diced
4 sprigs thyme
4 stalks Italian parsley
sea salt and freshly ground pepper

Dust chicken pieces lightly with flour. Melt oil and butter, add chicken and brown really well. Remove chicken, add leeks and cook for 10 minutes until soft. Add carrots and celery, and cook gently for 10 minutes. Add white wine and let bubble for 2 minutes. Add broth, tomatoes, potatoes, herbs, salt and pepper and heat through.

Return the chicken to the pan, and simmer over gentle heat for 1½ hours, turning chicken occasionally. Skim off any oil that may gather on the surface every now and then.

Serve with fresh thyme scattered on top.

Feeds four.

Chili con carne

This is one of those fast versions of the original that has grown to be a tradition in its own right. I have completely ignored all claims that these sorts of dishes don't have beans in them, because I like beans in them. I also have no idea if it should be spelt chili, chile, chilli, or chillie.

2 tbsp vegetable oil
2 onions, chopped
3 garlic cloves, crushed
1 kg (2 lb) minced beef or lamb
1 tbsp ground coriander
1 tsp ground cumin
1 bay leaf
1 tsp ground paprika
½ to 1 tsp ground chile powder, e.g. ancho
500 g (1 lb) canned tomatoes with juices
1 red pepper (capsicum), finely chopped
few sprigs of fresh oregano
1½ cups water
sea salt and freshly ground pepper
400 g (14 oz) canned red kidney beans, drained
1 packet corn chips

Heat oil in a heavy-bottomed pan and cook onions and garlic until golden. Add meat and cook for 10 minutes, stirring well, until browned. Add coriander, cumin, bay leaf, paprika and chile powder and cook for 5 minutes.

Add tomatoes, red pepper, oregano, water, salt and pepper. Bring to the boil, stirring, then simmer, covered, for an hour or until sauce thickens, stirring occasionally. Add drained red kidney beans and cook uncovered for 10 minutes, until thick and soupy. Taste for spices, salt and pepper, and adjust flavours accordingly.

Serve with a bowl of corn chips and a bowl of hot steamed rice (Pantry, 214).

Feeds four.

Pasta

Pasta is not something to cook when you can't be bothered cooking.

It is a benevolently noble dish, requiring imagination, perfect timing, and quality ingredients of the utmost freshness.

Nor is pasta a noodle. Noodles are noodles.

Fresh pasta is fast, simple, healthy, and easy to eat and digest.

Dried, it is tough and resilient, taking longer to cook, longer to absorb the sauce, and longer to eat.

This is how pasta should be, not overcooked, overdrained, oversauced or overloaded.

A good pasta sauce shouldn't have any more than two or three main ingredients

(and smoked chicken, lemongrass or soy sauce should never be one of them).

You should be able to cook a great sauce in the time it takes to cook the pasta.

The world does not need coloured pasta (or flavoured coffee, come to think of it) because it's silly.

Colour should come from the sauce, which should change with the seasons.

In Spring, think baby vegetables; in autumn, mushrooms, cured meats and olives; in winter, long-cooked meat sauces, and in summer, seafood, tomatoes, basil or fresh cheeses.

Pasta absorbs enormous quantities of sauce (the hotter it is, the more it soaks up),

so always reserve a ladleful of the pasta cooking water in case you need it.

Buy your Parmigiano – glorious, grainy, mouth-filling – in a piece, chipped in a wedge directly from a well-aged round, and grate it at the table, directly onto your pasta.

Store Parmigiano in the refrigerator, wrapped first in cheesecloth, and secondly in foil or plastic – but don't use it over delicate seafood sauces.

If you never have, then now is the time to make your own pasta, because it feels good, tastes good, costs less, is a worthwhile skill to learn, is more fun than doing weights at the gym, cooks faster than dried pasta, and can be turned into cannelloni, tortellini, or lasagne.

But mainly because you're not allowed to muck around with play-dough any more.

Sophia Loren knew the power of pasta. 'Everything you see' she once said, 'I owe to spaghetti'.

We all owe a lot to spaghetti.

Pasta

A nice ragù
Fresh egg pasta
Penne with tomato and basil
Pumpkin ravioli
Pappardelle with chicken livers
Pasta con primizie
Rigatoni timballo
Bigoli with anchovy sauce
Maccherone with sweet ricotta
Pasta alla carbonara
Orecchiette with cauliflower
Pasta e piselli

A nice ragù

It's all we need in life, isn't it? Just a nice ragù, based on the classic long-cooked meat sauce of Bologna, which was always a real ragù (stew) rather than the sauce we have come to know on 'spaghetti Bolognese'. Serve it over wide-cut pappardelle or stracci, layer it into a lasagne or spoon it over soft, fresh strichetti (fresh egg pasta, this page).

1 onion
1 celery stalk
1 carrot, peeled
1 garlic clove
100 g (3½ oz) pancetta or bacon
2 tbsp olive oil
500 g (1 lb) veal, cut into cubes
1 tsp plain, all-purpose flour
sea salt and freshly ground black pepper
½ tsp ground nutmeg
½ cup dry white wine
2 cups meat or chicken broth
300 g (11 oz) canned tomatoes and juice
2 tbsp tomato paste (concentrate)
1 sprig rosemary
3 sprigs thyme
500 g (1 lb) pasta
1 tsp butter
1 tbsp finely chopped parsley
Parmigiano for grating

Chop onion, celery, carrot, garlic and pancetta finely. Heat olive oil in a large frypan and cook mixture until it softens. Add veal and cook, stirring so that it breaks up and doesn't stick, until it is lightly browned.

Remove veal from pan, chop it finely, and return to pan. Add flour, salt, pepper and nutmeg and stir through. Turn up the heat, add white wine and let it bubble and evaporate until very little is left.

Add broth, tomatoes and their juice, tomato paste, rosemary and thyme and simmer over a low heat for an hour or so.

Cook pasta in plenty of boiling, salted water until al dente. Drain pasta and combine with sauce in a warm serving bowl. Top with butter and parsley and serve with Parmigiano.

Feeds four.

Fresh egg pasta

You know your life is working when you can get up on Sunday morning, make your own pasta, then sit down and eat it for lunch. The pushing and shoving is hard slog for a few minutes, but it's one of the most rewarding kitchen activities I know.

2 cups durum wheat flour or plain flour
2 eggs (60 g)
1 tbsp extra virgin olive oil

Make a deep crater in a mound of flour. Break 2 eggs into the centre. Add olive oil and gently beat with a fork, slowly drawing in more and more flour until all flour has been absorbed. Knead for 10 minutes in your hands, pushing the dough away from you with the heel of your palms, drawing it back, and turning it constantly, until it is no longer floury but smooth and shiny. Roll it into a ball, cover in plastic wrap and rest for 30 minutes.

Roll out dough with a rolling pin (hard work), or put it through a pasta machine four or five times, starting with the widest setting, and changing it to progressively smaller settings (easy work). Cut the pasta into long, thin strips (tagliatelle/fettuccine) by hand or by guiding it through the cutting attachment on the machine. Hang to dry for an hour or so on a wooden rack in a cool place.

Cook pasta in a large pot of simmering, salted water until al dente, tender but firm to the bite. Drain and combine with the sauce of your choice.

P.S. To make pappardelle, roll to the thinnest setting and cut by hand into 2 cm (¾ in) wide strips. Serve with the nice ragù (this page). To make strichetti, cut into 5 cm by 2.5 cm (2 in by 1 in) rectangles and pinch in the centres to form a bow. Serve in a soup or with the nice ragù (this page).

Feeds six.

Penne with tomato and basil

I wish I had invented this. It's quite simply the best pasta sauce in the world. It's not one of the oldest, because tomatoes didn't hit Italy until the end of the sixteenth century, but they certainly made up for lost time. Even miserable out-of-season tomatoes are improved with this treatment, so summer's best become truly heavenly.

1 kg (2 lb) ripe, red tomatoes
6 tbsp olive oil
2 garlic cloves, lightly smashed
½ tsp sea salt
1 tsp sugar
1 bunch basil
500 g (1 lb) penne

Dunk tomatoes in a pot of boiling water for 15 seconds, remove and peel off skin. Cut in half and squeeze out seeds. Chop remaining tomato flesh roughly.

Gently heat olive oil, tomatoes, garlic, salt and sugar and half the basil leaves and cook gently until soft, around 30 minutes.

Cook pasta in plenty of simmering, salted water until tender, but still firm to the bite. Drain well, and divide between 4 warmed pasta plates.

Add remaining basil leaves to the tomato sauce, heat through quickly and spoon on top of the pasta.

Feeds four.

Pumpkin ravioli

A variation on the splendid dish from Lombardy (where it is usually served as tortelli or as large tortelloni), which exploits pumpkin's natural sweetness. The main trick is to bake a lot of the moisture out of the pumpkin before mixing it into the filling. Save this for people you really, really like.

500 g (1 lb) pumpkin, in one piece, with skin
1 small egg
2 tbsp breadcrumbs
6 crushed amaretti biscuits
½ tsp nutmeg
½ cup grated Parmigiano
sea salt and freshly ground black pepper
400 g (14 oz) fresh pasta (Pasta, 102)
4 tbsp clarified butter (Pantry, 217)
fresh sage leaves

Heat oven to 180°C (350°F). Bake the pumpkin in 2 or 3 large pieces until tender (about 1 hour). Remove the skin and seeds, and purée flesh until smooth. Add egg, breadcrumbs, biscuits, nutmeg, cheese, and salt to taste.

Divide the pasta dough in half, and roll out one half on a floured board until thin. Cut into 2 equal-sized sheets. Place heaped teaspoons of filling about 8 cm (3 in) apart. Cover with the second sheet and press firmly between the mounds of filling. Cut with a pastry wheel into plump, square little cushions. Continue until you have 6 ravioli per person.

Boil ravioli in a large saucepan of salted, boiling water for 3 or 4 minutes, until they have all risen to the surface and pasta is tender. Drain well and divide ravioli between six warmed pasta plates. Melt butter and sage in a small frypan until it just starts to turn nutty and golden, and drizzle over ravioli. Serve with extra grated cheese.

Feeds six.

Pappardelle with chicken livers

These wide, generous ribbons of pasta go well with feisty Tuscan sauces like braised goat, hare, and this quick sauté of tomato, chicken livers and rosemary. Make this only when you find fresh, firm, clean-looking chicken livers, which is generally where you will find fresh, firm, clean-looking chickens.

400 g (14 oz) chicken livers
2 tbsp olive oil
2 garlic cloves, flattened
1 small onion, finely chopped
1 tsp rosemary leaves
a few sage leaves
½ cup red wine
1 cup tomato passato (purée not paste)
sea salt and freshly ground black pepper
500 g (1 lb) pappardelle or tagliatelle (page 102)
1 tbsp butter
Parmigiano for grating

Wash and trim the livers, removing any icky membrane and discolourations, and cut into 2.5 cm (1 in) pieces. Heat olive oil, add garlic, and cook for 2 minutes. Add onion and cook until soft. Add livers, rosemary and sage, and cook, stirring, until livers are almost cooked, about 3 minutes.

Remove livers, turn up heat, add wine, and allow sauce to bubble and reduce. Add tomato passato or sauce, and cook for 10 minutes until sauce thickens. Taste for salt and pepper. Cook pasta in plenty of boiling, salted water until al dente.

Return the livers to the pan and heat through for a minute or two. Drain pasta and toss with butter in a warmed serving bowl. Pour sauce on top, toss and serve with grated cheese.

Feeds four.

Pasta con primizie

The first, early cropping of the fruit and vegetable harvest – known as *primizie* – were revered throughout Italy in ancient festivals and feasting. Make this pasta as soon as you see the first small peas, asparagus, beans, artichoke hearts, broad beans or sugar snap peas. Yes, it does sound a lot like pasta primavera, but that was created relatively recently, by Sirio Maccioni of New York's Le Cirque restaurant in 1975.

20 small thin asparagus spears
4 ripe tomatoes
handful of green beans
1 cup peas, shelled
4 tbsp olive oil
2 garlic cloves, crushed
1 small onion, finely chopped
1 zucchini, cut into small cubes
sea salt and freshly ground black pepper
1 cup vegetable or chicken broth
500 g (1 lb) fettuccine
1 tbsp chopped parsley
1 tbsp chopped mint
extra virgin olive oil

Trim asparagus by snapping and discarding ends. Cut into short lengths. Dunk tomatoes into a pot of boiling water for 10 seconds. Remove, peel, cut in half, squeeze out seeds and cut flesh into small dice. Trim beans and cut on the diagonal. Cook peas in simmering salted water for 10 minutes until tender. Drain and rinse under cold running water and set aside.

Heat olive oil, add garlic and onion and cook for 5 minutes. Add zucchini, asparagus, and beans and cook for 5 minutes, stirring. Add tomatoes, peas, broth, salt and pepper and cook for 10 minutes, stirring.

Cook pasta in plenty of boiling, salted water until al dente. Drain and combine with sauce in a warmed serving bowl. Add parsley and mint, and serve immediately, drizzled with a little extra virgin olive oil.

Serve with a wedge of Parmigiano cheese to grate at the table.

Feeds four.

Rigatoni timballo

This elegant baked dish is based on the Sicilian 'pasta 'ncaciata', a magnificent mound of hard-boiled eggs, cheese, pasta and tomato sauce encased in a shell of eggplant. It's very showy, especially when the knife pierces the eggplant shell at the table, and the rich filling tumbles out in a cloud of steam and good smells.

3 medium-sized eggplants (aubergines)
salt
2 tbsp light olive oil
500 g (1 lb) rigatoni, penne, or maccheroni
500 g (1 lb) tomatoes, peeled, seeded and chopped
 or 600 g (1¼ lb) canned tomatoes with their juices
2 cups tomato passato (purée not paste)
sea salt and freshly ground black pepper
6 bocconcini balls (fresh mozzarella), sliced
3 hard-boiled eggs, quartered
½ cup grated Parmigiano

Slice eggplant lengthwise into 1 cm (½ in) slices. Sprinkle with salt, and leave for 1 hour. Pat dry with paper towel.

Heat oil in large frypan, and fry eggplant, a few slices at a time until golden brown, or grill until tender. Drain on paper towel and set aside.

Heat oven to 190°C (375°F). Cook pasta in plenty of salted boiling water until al dente, tender but still firm to the bite. Combine tomatoes, tomato passato, salt and pepper in saucepan and heat, stirring. Drain pasta well and combine with tomato sauce.

Arrange a layer of cooked eggplant on the lightly oiled base and sides of a 2.5 litre (4 pint) heatproof bowl or soufflé dish, overlapping the sides slightly. Fill with some of the pasta and sauce, then arrange half the bocconcini cheese and quartered eggs in a layer. Top with more pasta and sauce, and another layer of cheese and eggs. Finish with remaining pasta and sauce, and arrange remaining eggplant on top, tucking in any overlapping eggplant from the sides. Cover with foil and bake for 30 to 40 minutes.

Remove foil and loosen the timballo with a knife. Place a large warmed serving platter on top of the dish and carefully turn the entire thing over so that the moulded eggplant slips out onto the platter.

Serve at the table, with a green salad.

Feeds six.

Bigoli with anchovy sauce

In the Veneto, this extra-large wholewheat spaghetti is served with a sauce of sweet onion and salty anchovy and lots of freshly ground black pepper. A wildly sophisticated layering of flavour sensations that is custom-built for a simple supper.

1 tbsp butter
2 tbsp olive oil
2 onions, sliced
8 anchovy fillets in olive oil
500 g (1 lb) bigoli or bucatini pasta
freshly ground black pepper
1 tbsp chopped parsley

Heat butter and olive oil in a large frypan, add onions and cook gently until soft. Add anchovy fillets and stir until they break up.

Cook the pasta in plenty of salted, boiling water until al dente. Drain well, and mix with the sauce in a warm serving bowl, adding a few spoonfuls of the cooking water to moisten it. Add freshly ground black pepper and the parsley, and serve immediately.

Feeds four.

Maccherone with sweet ricotta

Early Roman *maccherone* dishes were made by rolling the pasta around knitting needles, and were often sauced with a little sugar, cinnamon and ricotta cheese, and served as a first course. Bizarre, yes, but wait until you try it.

400 g (14 oz) macaroni
sea salt
300 g (11 oz) fresh ricotta cheese
2 tbsp plain yoghurt
1 tbsp caster sugar
½ tsp ground cinnamon
½ tsp ground nutmeg

Cook pasta in a large pot of simmering, salted water until al dente, tender but firm to the bite.

Mix ricotta, yoghurt, sugar, cinnamon and nutmeg together in a large bowl and beat well. Add 3 or 4 tablespoons of pasta cooking water and beat until creamy. Drain pasta and tip into the sauce, tossing well. Dust generously with extra ground nutmeg, and serve immediately.

Feeds four.

Pasta alla carbonara

This has become almost as much of a cliché as spag bol, and for the same damn fine reason: it's a great dish. Named for the coal-burners (*i carbonari*) of Rome, the amount of black pepper is said to be reminiscent of a typical charcoal-carrier's meal – the little black bits presumably having fallen into the dish. I add a little cream to the original, but you probably shouldn't.

4 egg yolks
2 tbsp thickened (whipping) cream
2 tbsp grated Parmigiano
sea salt and freshly ground black pepper
500 g (1 lb) spaghetti or tagliatelle
4 thin slices of bacon, diced

Beat egg yolks in a bowl. Beat in the cream, cheese, salt, and lots of black pepper, and set aside.

Cook pasta in plenty of boiling, salted water until al dente. Fry bacon in a non-stick pan until crisp. Drain off a little of the bacon fat if you like. Drain pasta and toss immediately with the bacon, then combine with the egg mixture while it is still very hot. Toss quickly, to allow the heat of the spaghetti to cook the egg into a creamy cheese sauce. Serve on warm plates and rush to the table.

Feeds four.

Orecchiette with cauliflower

In Southern Italy, even the pasta has ears. Cauliflower tossed with olives, strengthened with chilli and linked with the ubiquitous tomato is a good match for the ear-shaped orecchiette. The much-maligned broccoli is also magnificent done in this manner. When cooking Sicilian or Sardinian pasta dishes that require cheese, try using grated pecorino at the table rather than the more northern Parmigiano, for the flavour of the deep south.

500 g (1 lb) cauliflower
3 tbsp olive oil
1 onion, finely sliced into rings
300 g (11 oz) ripe or canned tomatoes
500 g (1 lb) orecchiette
sea salt and freshly ground black pepper
4 anchovy fillets
1 red chilli, sliced
½ cup mild black olives, stoned and sliced
1 tbsp freshly chopped parsley
2 tbsp grated Parmigiano or pecorino

Cut cauliflower into small tree-like florets and cook in a little salted, boiling water for 3 minutes. Drain and keep warm.

Heat 2 tablespoons of the olive oil in a frypan, add onion and cook until soft but still pale. Add tomatoes, salt and pepper and simmer for a few minutes. Add cauliflower, cover, and cook very gently for 10 minutes.

Cook pasta in plenty of boiling, salted water until al dente.

Heat remaining olive oil in a small frypan, add anchovies and chilli, and cook for 2 minutes. Add to sauce with olives and parsley, and stir gently. Drain pasta well, tip into a warmed serving bowl and mix with sauce. Sprinkle with grated cheese and serve.

Feeds four.

Pasta e piselli

Fresh green peas, pasta, sweet onion and prosciutto are sympathetically linked in this juicy Italian dish, served in a soupy style with spoon and fork. It is even more delicious served with freshly made pasta, cut into strips and then into small squares, but it is perfectly acceptable to use any good small dried pasta or broken-up sheets of dried lasagne.

2 tbsp olive oil
1 onion, finely sliced into rings
4 slices prosciutto or pancetta, cut into strips
2 cups peas
1 litre (1¾ pints) chicken broth, hot
1 cup small dried pasta or broken-up lasagne
handful of fresh basil leaves, chopped
sea salt and freshly ground black pepper
1 tsp butter

Heat olive oil, and fry onion until soft but not browned. Add prosciutto and peas and toss well. Pour hot chicken broth on top, and cook for 10 minutes until peas are cooked.

Cook pasta in plenty of simmering, salted water until tender. Drain and add pasta to the broth. Add basil, salt and pepper to taste, and cook for 5 minutes or so, stirring occasionally, until pasta is soft.

Serve immediately, adding a little butter to each dish for a touch of richness.

Feeds four.

Don't you just love 'em?

The long, spindly ones like tree roots, the creamy fat ones like baby's knees, the tiny plump ones like eggs in a nest,

and the huge nobbly ones like old men's noses.

Don't you just adore them mashed with a little butter and hot milk,

roasted with rosemary and garlic,

boiled and tossed with fresh mint in a warm potato salad,

baked with blue cheese until crisp, brown and bubbling,

cooked slowly with a spoonful of duck fat,

finely sliced and roasted into paper-thin crisps,

baked into an edible crust on luscious stews,

formed into soft pillows of potato gnocchi and tossed with sage leaves frizzled in butter,

layered with big, fat anchovy fillets and baked until steaming,

fried in thick slices into a Spanish tortilla,

teamed with sweet onion,

whipped into soft nuts of salt cod and fried until crisp and golden,

puréed with leeks into a velvety vichyssoise soup,

spiced with mustard seeds and pan-fried with cauliflower,

baked in the oven just covered with rich chicken broth,

sandwiched with winter truffles and served with Champagne,

mashed under grilled sausages and crisp-fried onion rings,

tossed while steaming hot into a sharp vinaigrette and served with warm poached chicken,

cooked long and slow into a buttery French *pommes fondantes*,

grated and fried into golden pancakes,

mashed with green onions into an Irish colcannon, or just plain boiled, and eaten with a little dob of butter?

Or a large dob of caviar.

Potatoes make me want to stay home for tea, help myself to seconds, drink more wine, turn up the music,

and write really long sentences.

Potatoes should only taste of themselves, or better.

Avoid them only when they are over-irrigated and tasteless.

Or when they turn a toxic solanine green before you can get close enough to cook them.

Or when they are piped into fancy shapes and stiffened with egg yolk, or stuffed with cheap cheese and tasting of silver foil.

A good, well-flavoured, well-cooked potato is one of the new luxuries of the world.

You can live without them, but only if you really, really, really like rice.

Potatoes

Perfect mash
Indian spiced potatoes
Potato and bacon omelette
Potato, feta and walnut salad
Shepherd's pie
Potato roesti with caviar
Colcannon
Stoemp and smoked ham

Perfect mash

The trick to perfect mash is to not let the potatoes absorb too much water (cook them unpeeled and uncut), and to dry them well – in the drained pan over gentle heat – before mashing. The other trick is to use hot milk instead of cold, which gives a sweet lusciousness that makes people swear you have used cream.

4 medium potatoes: nicola, pontiac, pink eye, King Edward
sea salt
1/2 cup milk, heated
1 tbsp butter, very cold
sea salt and freshly ground black pepper

Cover potatoes with cold water, and salt generously. Bring to the boil and simmer gently for 30 minutes until potatoes are evenly cooked. Drain and peel potatoes as soon as you can manage it without burning yourself (the hotter, the better).

Return peeled potatoes to the hot pan over a gentle heat for a moment or two to absorb any excess moisture. Mash well, removing pan from heat if it gets too dry. Add hot milk, beating with a wooden spoon. Cut butter into tiny dice and add a few dice at a time, beating continuously, until potato feels smooth and has a light sheen. Add sea salt and pepper to taste, and stir well. Serve immediately.

P.S. Or swap the butter for extra virgin olive oil, and infuse the milk by heating it with some smashed garlic, finely diced onion, a few saffron threads, or green (spring) onions. For a chlorophyll-green parsley mash, whizz blanched parsley leaves with butter and milk and beat them into the mashed potato.

Feeds four.

Indian spiced potatoes

A charming, well balanced Indian recipe that combines potatoes with cauliflower, adapted from a recipe by the charming and well balanced Indian food authority Madhur Jaffrey. When you are looking for what are called black mustard seeds, remember they are brown, but don't ask me why.

1/2 cauliflower
3 medium potatoes, peeled
4 tbsp peanut oil
1 tbsp black mustard seeds
8 curry leaves
1 green chilli, chopped or 1/2 tsp chilli powder
1/2 tsp ground turmeric
1/2 tsp ground coriander
1/2 tsp ground cumin
1/2 tsp salt
1/2 tsp sugar
250 ml (9 fl oz) water
2 tbsp chopped fresh coriander

Cut cauliflower into small florets until you have around 2 cups worth. Cut potatoes into small dice. Cook potatoes and cauliflower in a large pot of simmering, salted water for 2 minutes, then drain well and set aside.

Warm oil in frypan until hot. Add black mustard seeds and stir while they pop, then add curry leaves. Stir through, then add chilli, turmeric, coriander, cumin, salt and sugar. Cook, stirring, for 1 minute, then add drained potatoes and cauliflower, and toss well.

Add water and bring to the boil, stirring. Cover and lower heat. Cook gently for at least 15 minutes, stirring occasionally, or until potatoes are tender and dish is almost dry, just linked with the juices. Sprinkle with fresh coriander and serve with plenty of rice.

Feeds four.

Potato and bacon omelette

A hearty, rustic meal originally designed to fill and satisfy a body that had worked since daybreak. It also works quite well on a sedentary body that's been at a computer screen all day.

4 small potatoes, cooked
4 slices of bacon, speck or kaiserfleisch
8 eggs
sea salt and freshly ground pepper
1 tbsp dry white wine

Cut potatoes into thick slices. Cut rind from bacon and cut bacon into small squares.

Fry bacon in a large (25 cm or 10 in diameter) frypan over gentle heat until fat melts and bacon is cooked but not crisp. Remove bacon and pour off most of the fat. Add potato slices and fry on both sides until golden brown.

Beat eggs with salt, pepper and wine, until lightly mixed. Return bacon to pan, then pour in the eggs and cook over gentle heat for 5 minutes, lifting the potato slices up to allow egg to run beneath them and set.

Use a knife to pull back the edges of the setting omelette and tip the pan to spill the more liquid egg into the space so that it will also set, and cook until the bottom has set and the top is slightly liquid.

Fold one half of the omelette over on top of the other half, so that the heat cooks the remaining unset egg, and don't worry if it starts to fall apart and look messy, which it probably will.

Turn the whole lot out on to a warm platter, cut into two or four sections, and serve with a green salad.

Feeds two to four.

Potato, feta and walnut salad

This modern-looking salad is from the cutting edge of ancient civilisation. Soft, fresh cheese and walnuts have won hearts since the two were first paired in ancient Greece. Seek out the finest and freshest sheep's milk feta or any soft, fresh curd-like cheese.

4 waxy potatoes (e.g. nicola)
2 tbsp red wine vinegar
1 tsp Dijon mustard
sea salt and freshly ground black pepper
4 tbsp extra virgin olive oil
baby lamb's lettuce or the tips of curly endive
200 g (7 oz) fresh feta cheese
4 tbsp walnuts, roughly chopped

Cook potatoes in simmering salted water for 30 minutes. Cool, peel and cut into thick slices.

Combine vinegar, mustard, sea salt and pepper in a bowl and slowly whisk in olive oil. Taste, and adjust accordingly. Toss lamb's lettuce and walnuts in dressing.

Arrange a layer of potato slices on serving plates and drizzle with any remaining dressing. Top with blocks of feta cheese, and top with dressed leaves and walnuts.

Feeds four.

Shepherd's pie

If it uses minced uncooked lamb, it's a shepherd's pie, and if it uses leftover cooked beef, it's cottage pie. Coming from a sheep farm, I prefer the former, and I also add an untraditional layer of home-cooked, jammy tomato sauce under the potato. Serve with a huge bowl of fresh peas, and you will win over young and old.

2 tbsp butter
2 onions, finely chopped
2 garlic cloves, crushed
500 g (1 lb) minced lamb
1 tbsp flour
4 tomatoes, chopped
1 bay leaf
2 tbsp finely chopped parsley
sea salt and freshly ground black pepper
4 potatoes
3 tbsp milk
½ cup tomato jam (Pantry, 219)
1 tbsp butter, for potato topping

Heat butter and cook onions and garlic for 10 minutes. Add minced lamb and cook, stirring, until browned. Sprinkle flour on top of meat and stir well, allowing flour to cook. Add tomatoes, bay leaf and parsley and cook for 20 minutes, stirring occasionally. Feel free to add a little water as it cooks, if necessary, to create more of a sauce. Taste for salt and pepper and adjust accordingly.

Peel potatoes and cook in simmering, salted water until tender. Drain and return briefly to the heat to dry out any excess moisture. Mash thoroughly, adding milk, salt and pepper.

Pour meat sauce into a lightly oiled one-litre (1¾ pint) pie dish, top with tomato jam if desired, and spread a thick layer of mashed potato on top. Add a few little dobs of butter on top, and bake for 30 minutes, until potato is crisp and brown on top and meat is hot.

Feeds four.

Potato roesti with caviar

The first trick to these Swiss grated potato pancakes not to overcook the potatoes when boiling them. The second trick is to boil them the day before, and leave them uncovered in the refrigerator to dry out. The third trick is to top them with sour cream and either the best caviar you can afford or a few smoked salmon shavings.

500 g (1 lb) peeled potatoes
1 egg, beaten
pinch of salt
3 tbsp olive oil
4 tbsp light sour cream
50 g (2 oz) top-grade Iranian or salmon caviar

Cook the potatoes in simmering, salted water for about 10 minutes, or until a skewer inserted into the potato meets with no resistance until it gets to the middle, which should still be firm. Drain and allow to cool. Peel off skins, and refrigerate, preferably overnight.

Grate the potatoes into long strips. Add the beaten egg, salt, and one teaspoon of the oil, and mix lightly.

Heat remaining oil in a heavy-based frypan. When hot but not smoking, add two tablespoons of grated potato mixture, and press softly with an egg slice. Fry on both sides until golden brown, and drain on paper towel. Repeat with remaining potato mixture.

Allow to cool for a few minutes, then top with sour cream and a spoonful of caviar.

P.S. To be traditional about it, you would cook one big potato cake, using all the grated potato in the one pan. When the first side is golden brown, turn it out gently onto a flat plate and slide back into the pan to finish browning the other side. Cut into wedges to serve.

Feeds six.

Colcannon

The end of the harvest in Ireland was always celebrated with a meatless meal on October 31st, known as All Hallow Eve (Halloween), and colcannon is just one of the many potato dishes devised not just to feed but to satisfy. Traditionally, it was served with a pool of melted butter in the centre, but I find it rich enough without it. Well, maybe just a little dob.

500 g (1 lb) Savoy cabbage
500 g (1 lb) potatoes
6 green (spring) onions
125 ml (4 fl oz) cream
125 ml (4 fl oz) milk
sea salt and freshly ground black pepper
1 tsp butter

Cut cabbage into thin shreds and rinse well in a pot of cold water. Cook cabbage in a large pot of simmering salted water until just tender, and drain well. Peel potatoes and cook in simmering, salted water until tender.

Chop green onions finely. Heat green onions, cream and milk in a small pot, stirring, and simmer gently for 5 minutes.

Mash potatoes well, then start beating with a wooden spoon, gradually introducing the cream and onions. Add sea salt and pepper and stir well. Add cabbage, stir once or twice and serve topped with – a little – butter.

Feeds four.

Stoemp and smoked ham

A Belgian potato dish (pronounced stoomp) of mashed potatoes and greens such as leeks or spinach, traditionally served with sausages, fish or fried onions. I particularly like it with a quickly grilled slice of lightly smoked pork or even ham off the bone.

6 potatoes
2 leeks
1 tbsp butter
sea salt and freshly ground black pepper
pinch of grated nutmeg
4 thick slices kasseler, speck or smoked pork

Peel potatoes and cut into quarters. Cut off the white outer leaves of leek until you reach the green centre leaves, and slice into very fine rings. Rinse well in a large pot of cold water, and set aside.

Cook potatoes in simmering, salted water for 20 minutes or until tender. Add leeks for one last minute of cooking, then drain. Return briefly to the heat to dry out any excess moisture. Remove from heat, add butter, salt, pepper and nutmeg and mash lightly.

Cook smoked pork on or under a hot grill until sizzling.

Divide stoemp between four warmed serving plates and top with grilled smoked pork.

Feeds four.

Vegetables are revolting.

No longer content to be set on the side of meat, they have taken centre stage.

Think about what vegetable you would like for dinner, rather than what meat.

Then grill eggplant (aubergine), zucchini, red, green and yellow peppers (capsicums), brushed with herbed olive oil.

Roast beetroot, potatoes, sweet potatoes, pumpkin, carrots, parsnips.

Boil artichokes, asparagus, beans, peas, cabbages, cauliflower.

Fry eggplant, zucchini, potatoes and parsnip, cut very finely into vegetable chips.

Steam Chinese cabbage, cauliflower, sweet corn and broccoli, and serve drizzled with a little soy sauce and sesame oil.

Mash celeriac, pumpkin, potato, parsnip and carrot with butter, a little cream, and nutmeg.

Or just eat fennel, mushrooms, radishes, asparagus and carrots raw, finely sliced and tossed in red wine vinegar, extra virgin olive oil, salt, pepper and chopped parsley.

We should be able to get home any night of the week, put a frypan on the stove, add olive oil and garlic, and then look in the refrigerator to decide what to cook.

At the very least, add finely diced, peeled potato, pumpkin and twigs of fresh rosemary and gently fry until vegetables are crisp and golden.

Eat the roots, stems and leaves of vegetables, not just the pretty part. (But not the leaves of tomato, rhubarb and potato plants, we don't need to lose another good cook.)

And don't laugh at funny coloured vegetables: until the Dutch started breeding carrots for colour and sweetness in the seventeenth century, all carrots were purple.

The future of our food supply depends on horticultural and agricultural diversity – the more limited the gene pool, the more susceptible the food supply is to environmental change and new disease: so eat lots of different vegetables.

But don't eat vegetables because they are good for you.

Nor because they leave you feeling satisfied but not weighed down.

Nor even because they are so easy to cook into a variety of seductive dinners.

Eat them for one reason alone.

Because they're *gorgeous*.

Vegetables

Celeriac purée
Fennel schnitzel
Broad beans with prosciutto
Braised artichokes with basil and mint
Belacan spinach
Vegetable chips
Gai laan with oyster sauce
Grilled asparagus with olives
Cauliflower cheese
Wing bean laksa
Caponata
Sweet potato crumble

Celeriac purée

This boring, nubbly looking root from the Mediterranean is just an ugly form of beautiful celery, lending itself to dressed salads, gratins and simple creamy purées such as this. The flavour is a revelation to celeriac virgins, and can lead to infatuation, which will do neither you nor the celeriac any harm at all. Serve with roast pork, ham or lamb, or a simple fish dish, or introduce some hot chicken broth after mashing and turn into a dreamy soup, finished with cream.

1 celeriac
2 potatoes
sea salt and freshly ground black pepper
1 tbsp butter
3 tbsp thickened cream

Peel celeriac and potatoes and cut into small cubes. Place in saucepan and cover with cold water. Add salt, bring to the boil and simmer for 30 minutes. Drain well, and return to the heat for a moment to dry off any excess moisture. Add butter, and mash well, to a purée. Add cream, sea salt and plenty of black pepper, and beat well.

Feeds four.

Fennel schnitzel

In Italy, sweet aniseedy fennel used to be served at the end of the meal, as refreshing a concept as fresh fruit. Here, golden breadcrumbs give a crisp coating on fresh, zesty fennel, to be served with roast chicken or grilled fish, or just as part of an antipasto platter. This is also brilliant with thick slices of blanched celeriac, as another sort of vegetable schnitzel.

2 fennel bulbs
2 eggs
1 cup fine dry breadcrumbs
sea salt and black pepper
vegetable oil for frying

Trim tops of each fennel bulb, and cut off any nasty looking bits of outer skin. Cut down through the fennel bulbs into very thin, neat cross-sections. Rinse and pat dry.

Break eggs into one bowl and beat them lightly. Place breadcrumbs in a second bowl and season with salt and pepper. Heat oil, up to 2 cm (¾ in) deep, in a heavy-based frypan. Dip each fennel slice first in beaten egg, then in breadcrumbs, then fry, a few slices at a time, until golden, turning once. Drain on kitchen paper and sprinkle with a little sea salt.

Feeds six.

Broad beans with prosciutto

Known as 'the meat of the poor', broad beans are now the vegetable of the rich, double-shelled and gleaming green in their nakedness. I generally prefer them clothed because I love the flavour of the skin as much as the nutty bean itself, and because there is only so much peeling I can handle. Make your own choice with this recipe, which links them sympathetically with prosciutto and sweet onion.

1 kg (2 lb) broad beans
2 tbsp olive oil
2 tbsp finely chopped onion
4 slices prosciutto, finely chopped
sea salt and freshly ground black pepper
1 cup chicken broth
1 tbsp finely chopped parsley
extra virgin olive oil

Shell broad beans, and proceed with recipe, or cook in boiling, salted water for 10 minutes, then peel off skins and set aside.

Heat olive oil in a heavy-bottomed, non-reactive frypan, add onion and cook until soft but still white. Add prosciutto and cook for 1 minute. Add broad beans, salt, pepper and chicken broth, cover and cook gently for 15 minutes until beans are tender. Toss parsley through beans and serve in a warm bowl with a drizzle of olive oil on top, and lots of crusty bread nearby.

Feeds four as a side dish, or as a pasta sauce.

Braised artichokes with basil and mint

With this slow-cooking method, you can serve the artichokes warm or cold in the braising juices, quarter them and serve as a refreshing first course salad as pictured, or finish the dish by frying them until crisp.

20 small artichokes or 6 medium artichokes
1 lemon, halved
½ cup extra virgin olive oil
½ cup dry white wine
2 cups water
1 bay leaf
handful each of mint leaves, basil leaves and parsley leaves
2 anchovies, mashed
4 sundried tomatoes, sliced
freshly ground pepper
extra basil leaves

Cut the top 2 cm (¾ in) of the larger artichoke leaves away, and rub cut area with lemon. Remove a few of the tough outer leaves, and trim the stalks.

Combine olive oil, wine, water, bay leaf, mint, basil, parsley, anchovies and pepper with artichokes in a heavy-bottomed pan and bring to the boil. Cover partly, lower heat and cook gently for 1 hour, turning artichokes once or twice in that time.

Remove artichokes and boil until water evaporates and liquid is reduced to a very artichoke-flavoured oil. Cut artichokes into halves or quarters, stripping away any tough outer leaves or hairy inner choke. Spoon over the cooled juices and serve, dressed with a few fresh basil leaves and sundried tomatoes. Or fry artichoke halves or quarters in the oil until they are frizzled and crisp.

Feeds four.

Belacan spinach

Belacan, also known as (and pronounced) blachan, has a gloriously foul, dead-fishy stench – the street smell of Malaysia – giving you a real whiff of the wharves covered in trays of tiny salted, fermented shrimps all along the Malaysian coastline. When cooked, this dried shrimp paste has a rich, complex flavour and – thankfully – a more acceptable aroma. Serve as a side dish to char-grilled fish, a fiery Malaysian curry, steamed prawns, or fried noodles.

500 g (1 lb) fresh water spinach (kang kong)
2 dried red chillies, soaked and drained
2 garlic cloves
2 candlenuts or macadamia nuts
6 shallots or 1 small onion, chopped
2 tsp belacan (dried shrimp paste)
1 tbsp dried shrimps, ground
1 tbsp vegetable oil
½ tsp sugar

Wash water spinach and shake dry. Grind, pound or blend drained chillies, garlic, nuts, shallots or onion, belacan and dried shrimps to a paste. Heat oil in wok or frypan, and fry paste until fragrant. Add spinach and toss to coat in paste. Add sugar as soon as the leaves start to wilt, and keep tossing until stems soften and leaves have wilted.

Feeds four.

Vegetable chips

Take ignored and abused vegetables like sweet potato, eggplant, beetroot and zucchini, and chip 'em into an elegant appetiser with drinks, or accessories to a simple grill. The frizzled leeks are also very cute on top of a vegetable or meat stew, unless you're still tired of seeing them so often on restaurant entrées.

1 large beetroot
1 large parsnip
1 zucchini
2 slim eggplants (aubergines)
1 sweet potato
1 leek
vegetable oil for deep frying
sea salt

Peel and slice vegetables lengthwise, as thinly as humanly possible. Cut the white part of the leek into one 6 cm (2½ in) section, cut in half lengthwise, and divide the layers. Cut each layer into very fine matchstick lengths (julienne). Drop leeks into a pot of boiling water for 1 minute to soften, then drain and dry thoroughly with paper towel.

Heat oil until a small square of bread will brown evenly in about 10 seconds. Add vegetable chips a few at a time, and fry until lightly golden and crisp. Fry beetroot last in case it colours the oil. Drain on paper towel and sprinkle lightly with sea salt. Fry leeks in small handfuls until crisp, and drain.

Arrange vegetable chips in a pile on a large platter and top with leeks.

Feeds four.

Gai laan with oyster sauce

I pinched this technique from the gai laan madame's trolley at yum cha. First, she blanches the cabbage in chicken broth, douses it with oyster sauce, and somehow manages to produce a platter of perfectly trimmed, neat cabbage, with glossy leaves on top and crunchy stems below, as the juices ooze out and mingle with the oyster sauce and create a light dressing. I can now do it at home, but it's not the same without the trolley.

500 g (1 lb) gai laan cabbage (Chinese broccoli)
1 slice ginger
1 garlic clove, smashed
1 litre (1¾ pints) water or chicken broth
2 tbsp oyster sauce

Wash and clean cabbage and chop into 5 cm (2 in) sections. Divide stems from the softer leaves, which will cook faster. Add ginger and garlic to a pot of simmering, salted water or chicken broth. Add cabbage stems and cook for 2 minutes until they just start to soften. Remove from water and drain in a colander. Add leaves and cook for up to 1 minute until they soften. Remove and drain in a colander.

Arrange a neat layer of stems on a warmed serving plate and top with a neat layer of leaves. Drizzle oyster sauce on top and serve immediately.

Feeds four as a side dish.

Grilled asparagus with olives

According to seventeenth-century teacher and publisher Giacomo Castelvetro, asparagus 'cannot harm any part of the human body'. He was also very keen on sprinkling it with bitter orange juice once grilled, which wouldn't do any harm, either.

700 g (1½ lb) asparagus
2 tbsp extra virgin olive oil
sea salt and freshly ground black pepper
4 hard-boiled eggs
½ cup small black olives

Bend the fibrous ends of the asparagus, and they will snap naturally at the right point for trimming. Brush asparagus lightly with olive oil and sprinkle with salt and pepper. Heat a ribbed grill until hot, and grill asparagus for five to ten minutes, turning once, until tender.

Peel eggs and gently remove yolks from whites. Chop yolks and whites separately until finely diced. Cut the olive meat away from the stone, and finely chop.

Arrange grilled asparagus on a large platter. Scatter with a layer of egg white, then egg yolk, then black olive, so that the colours form a strong contrast. Drizzle with extra virgin olive oil.

Feeds four as a side dish.

Cauliflower cheese

Originally known in sixteenth-century England as a Cyprus colewart, then coleflower, the cauliflower has survived even the British habit of baking it with a cheese sauce. I know people who make this good, old-fashioned favourite for their dinner. I mean, for their *entire* dinner. I guess that's what boarding school does for you. Consider steaming it whole, and serving completely bathed in sauce.

1 cauliflower, around 800 g (1¾ lb)
salt
1 tbsp butter
1 tbsp plain flour
1 cup milk
sea salt and freshly ground black pepper
grated nutmeg
2 tbsp grated gruyère cheese
1 tsp sweet hot paprika

Cut cauliflower into large florets like the branches of a tree, or leave whole. Rinse well in cold water and shake dry. Cook in a big pot of simmering salted water for around 10 minutes for florets, 20 to 30 minutes for whole cauliflower, then drain. Heat oven to 180°C (350°F). Butter a baking dish, and pack the cauliflower florets in it, quite tightly, or place the whole cauliflower in the dish.

Melt butter until foaming in a small saucepan. Sprinkle with flour while stirring madly with a wooden spoon. Reduce heat and cook for 2 or 3 minutes. Add milk gradually, stirring, until you have a nice thick sauce. Thin out the sauce with a little extra milk to a pouring-cream consistency. Add salt, pepper, nutmeg and cheese, and cook gently for 5 minutes to melt the cheese.

Pour the sauce over the cauliflower and bake for 30 minutes until golden brown on top. Remove from oven, and sprinkle with paprika. Serve at the table, from the dish.

Feeds four.

Wing bean laksa

Is it a bean, or a frilled extra-terrestrial? The wing bean is loved throughout Asia, both for the climbing vines and flowers of the plant and for the flavour of the bean. If you come across them, slice them on the diagonal and throw into a stir-fry, or into your favourite Thai curry or Malaysian laksa soup. If you don't come across them, use normal earthling green beans instead.

1 tbsp vegetable oil
1 slice fresh ginger
1 kg (2 lb) wing beans
1 tbsp laksa paste (Pantry, 218)
¾ cup coconut milk
½ cup chicken broth
few sprigs coriander

Heat wok until hot. Add oil, and heat. Add ginger and cook for 1 minute. Add wing beans, and toss well for 5 minutes over medium heat. Remove wing beans, discard ginger, and add the laksa paste to the wok. Cook for 3 minutes, then add chicken broth and coconut milk, stirring well. Heat gently without boiling, stirring constantly, then return beans to the wok and cook until just tender.

Feeds six.

Caponata

Caponata began in the *caupona*, a special osteria in southern Italy serving cooked vegetables. History has it that sailors bought the vegetables while in port, then ate them flavoured with vinegar and sugar when at sea. The sweet-and-sour vegetable stew that evolved is lovely on its own, piled on garlicky toast, or served with grilled octopus or tuna.

2 eggplants (aubergines)
1 tsp salt
3 tbsp olive oil
2 extra tbsp olive oil
4 onions, roughly chopped
3 celery stalks, chopped
½ cup green olives, stoned
6 tomatoes, roughly chopped
sea salt and pepper
1 tbsp sugar
3 tbsp red wine vinegar
1 tbsp salted capers, rinsed
2 tbsp toasted pine nuts

Cut eggplants into thick slices, then into 1 cm (½ in) square cubes. Sprinkle with salt and leave for 1 hour to stand. Rinse well, drain and dry with paper towel. Heat 3 tablespoons of olive oil in a frying pan and fry eggplant until golden brown. Drain on paper towel.

Heat extra olive oil in a heavy-bottomed pan. Add onions and cook for 10 minutes until they start to soften. Add celery, green olives, tomatoes and salt and pepper. Cook for another 10 minutes. Add the sugar, vinegar, capers and eggplant. Cook for another 10 minutes until the taste of the vinegar is no longer sharp.

Serve at room temperature scattered with pine nuts and drizzled with extra virgin olive oil, with lots of bread.

Feeds four.

Sweet potato crumble

According to John Gerard's *Herball* (1597), this fluorescently orange tuber 'used to be eaten rosted in the ashes' then dressed with oil, vinegar and salt. 'Notwithstanding how they be dressed, they comfort, nourish and strengthen the body.' If you tire of roasting them in the ashes, try this humble crumble with a crisp and buttery breadcrumb topping. Make your own soft breadcrumbs by whizzing some good stale bread in the food processor.

3 large sweet potatoes
2 tbsp butter
½ tsp grated nutmeg
sea salt and freshly ground black pepper
1 cup soft, fresh breadcrumbs
1 tsp very finely chopped parsley

Peel and roughly chop sweet potatoes. Cook in simmering salted water until tender. Drain and return to the heat for a moment with one tablespoon of butter, nutmeg, salt and pepper, stirring. Blend in food processor or mash until smooth, and spoon into a medium-sized ovenproof baking dish.

Melt remaining tablespoon of butter in pan, and add the fresh breadcrumbs gradually, stopping when the butter has been fully absorbed. Add parsley, stirring with a wooden spoon.

Top sweet potato with breadcrumbs. Bake at 200°C (400°F) for 20 to 30 minutes until golden.

Feeds four as a side dish.

Good food makes you feel better.

But there are times when even a cup of tea seems too strong for your delicate stomach,

or you're in bed with a streaming cold,

or you've simply had far too many good meals and your body is crying out for a rest.

It needs what the Italians call food cooked 'in bianco', which means you can eat just about anything, as long as it is white.

Rice, for instance, cooked in chicken broth and served with a little butter and grated Parmigiano.

A little scrambled egg,

cold roast chicken,

mashed potato,

soft white Chinese noodles,

Cantonese congee (rice soup),

steamed dumplings in chicken broth.

Personally, I like to add a little colour to the sheets of whiteness, if I'm feeling up to it.

Like fresh tagliatelle with a little broth of spring vegetables.

Or a poached egg on a bed of wilted spinach scented with nutmeg,

chicken noodle soup served with soldiers of toast,

a freshly made ham sandwich with soft, white bread,

or a few spears of steamed asparagus

or green beans.

Your body will tell you what it wants, and what it can handle.

The real test is a small, shivery junket, wobbly milk jelly, or creamy rice pudding: if you can't finish that, then I'm sorry,

but you're really sick.

Keep up the liquids with freshly drawn water (no ice), herbal teas, and light broths.

Avoid fats, cooking with cheese, anything greasy or oily, spicy foods, offal, deep-fried foods, dried beans, hard-boiled eggs,

pastry, unripe fruits and vegetables, acidic tomatoes, coffee, icy cold or burning hot foods,

and excessive sweetness or sourness.

If you're tending someone else, feed them on time, every time, with a pretty tray that won't fall over in bed.

Fluff up their pillows, be nice, and if they really, really want strawberry ice cream with chocolate sprinkles and marshmallows,

don't argue.

Getting exactly what you want can be the best medicine of all.

Risotto al Parmigiano

Heat 6 cups of light chicken broth.

Melt 1 tbsp butter in a heavy-bottomed saucepan, add one finely chopped onion, and cook for 4 or 5 minutes until soft.

Add 300 g (11 oz) of unwashed Italian superfino rice (e.g. arborio) and coat it well in the buttery onion.

Add ¾ cup dry white wine, and let it hiss and sputter and be absorbed by the rice, while you stir.

Using a ladle, add half a cup of heated chicken broth to the rice, and stir carefully and calmly over medium heat.

When the broth has been absorbed by the rice, add another half cup of broth.

From now on, it is all in the timing.

Add stock by the ladle only when the previous broth has been absorbed by the rice.

Keep the rice moving in the pan.

If you go through a lot of broth quickly, your heat may be too high.

If the rice doesn't absorb the broth easily, your heat may be too low.

After 20 minutes, start tasting the rice, and cook for another 10 minutes until rice is cooked but not soft,

and there is a general creaminess to the sauce, neither soupy nor dry.

Turn off the heat, add sea salt and freshly ground pepper, 1 tbsp butter and 2 tbsp freshly grated Parmigiano,

and stir it through.

Cover and leave to rest for 3 or 4 minutes before serving.

Feeds four.

Pudding

Skip the main course.

I'm serious. Design the meal to go from a substantial and satisfying first course, straight to the main event.

You can have meat-and-veg any night, but you can't have sago pudding with coconut milk and palm sugar, or sticky jam pudding with clotted cream, or even a crusty fruit crumble with pouring custard.

Pudding is worth the sacrifice.

Besides, what is worse than bringing a gleaming, steaming golden pudding to the table only to have everyone groan with horror instead of delight?

You need a clear space on the table and in your stomach for a pudding, and you need a good, long walk afterwards, preferably straight to the armchair for an uninterrupted snooze.

Puddings are magic. Men love them. Kids love them. Even dogs love them.

They are treats, and we need treats.

They are unapologetically plump and warm and giving, and we need plump, warm and giving things in our lives.

They are constructions as artificial as film stars, and yet they are neither phony nor fraudulent.

They simply exist, like film stars, for no other reason than to give us pleasure.

I love the downhomeliness of all puddings, but I love steamed puddings best of all, because they do their own thing while you're eating whatever it is you're eating before you eat them.

There is something about steaming that cleanses, purifies and nurtures food.

No harsh flames disturb it, no searing hot pans rob it of all moisture and tenderness. Instead, the powerful, healing, non-invasive properties of steam relax the tension in your batter and alleviate the stress of the flour, milk and eggs.

This is the obvious reason for humanity's general craving for a good steamed pudding, apart from its equally obvious ability to create feelings of well being and euphoria among the most mean-spirited of people, and to enhance the quality of our lives beyond the limits we thought possible.

Traditionally, puddings were filling stodge, designed to be the last word at the end of a meal of more stodge.

But they don't have to be.

They can be light and fragrant, based on fresh fruit, and shy of sugar.

They can be delicate and complex, full of subtlety and surprise.

Then, of course, you can completely ruin them by serving them with buckets of cream.

Pudding

Granny's goo
Ma lai cake
Steamed treacle pudding
Summer fruit crumble
Sticky toffee pud
Greek rice pudding
Sago pudding
Sticky jam pudding

Granny's goo

That's what this sticky self-saucing chocolate pudding was called in our family. It's not haute cuisine, but it is very warming and filling, both physically and metaphorically. Serve with pouring custard (Broths and Sauces, 210).

125 g (4½ oz) self-raising flour
2 tbsp cocoa
pinch of salt
100 g (3½ oz) soft butter
100 g (3½ oz) caster sugar
4 eggs, lightly beaten
½ tsp vanilla extract
3 tbsp milk

Sauce
1 cup boiling water
100 g (3½ oz) soft brown sugar
2 tbsp cocoa

Heat oven to 180°C (350°F). Sift together flour, cocoa and salt.

Cream butter and sugar until pale. Beat in eggs, one at a time, and then vanilla. Fold in flour and milk alternately, mixing well. Spoon into a buttered ovenproof 18 cm (7 in) baking dish.

Pour boiling water over cocoa and brown sugar in a heatproof bowl, and stir until dissolved. Pour the sauce over the pudding, and bake for 40 to 50 minutes, until the top has formed a crust, the centre is cooked, and bottom is runny. Serve with pouring custard, cream, or ice cream.

Feeds four.

Ma lai cake

Personally, I only go to yum cha for this feather-light sponge with its warm, treacly fragrance. Sadly, it comes right at the end of the meal, so I am forced to eat my way through steamed har gau dumplings, fluffy char sieu buns, and some lotus-wrapped sticky rice before I get to it. Every time. Serve it freshly steamed and eat with chopsticks, or give it a chic western touch with a sticky toffee sauce made of palm sugar.

4 eggs, at room temperature
1 tbsp water
180 g (6½ oz) white sugar
1 tbsp golden syrup
150 g (5¼ oz) flour
1 tsp baking powder

Sauce
150 g (5¼ oz) dark brown palm sugar
¾ cup thickened cream
½ tsp vanilla essence
2 tbsp butter

Butter a round or square 15 cm (6 in) diameter cake tin, and line the bottom with enough doubled greaseproof paper to form 'handles' above the level of the tin. Make sure your cake tin fits within your steamer. Sift flour and baking powder together and set aside.

Place eggs, water, sugar and golden syrup in food processor and blend for 10 minutes at high speed, until mixture is thick and creamy. Remove to a bowl, then fold in sifted flour and baking powder. Pour batter into the cake tin, and set inside the steamer over boiling water. Cover and steam for 30 to 40 minutes, keeping an eye on the water to make sure it doesn't boil dry. Insert a thin skewer to test if cake is cooked. If skewer comes out dry, not wet, and cake is cratered with small air bubbles, gently lift the cake from the tin using the greaseproof paper, rest on a rack and peel off paper.

Cut pudding into squares or wedges and place each serving in the centre of a warm dinner plate. Serve as is, in the Chinese style, or combine palm sugar, cream, vanilla essence and butter in a saucepan, bring to the boil, stirring, and simmer for 5 minutes. Pour hot sauce over each square, and serve.

Feeds four.

Steamed treacle puddings

Golden syrup is a yummy, sweet syrup of the treacle variety, popular in England and throughout the British Commonwealth. It can be replaced with a light corn syrup which will have a more subtle effect. Always use a hot spoon to measure out sweet syrups and honey, or most of it will stick to the spoon. Then it will stick to the kitchen bench. Then you. This is the real reason most of these puddings are known as sticky puddings.

4 tbsp golden syrup
140 g (5 oz) butter
140 g (5 oz) soft brown sugar
2 eggs
2 tbsp milk
140 g (5 oz) self-raising flour

Heat oven to 180°C (350°F). Butter four 200ml (7 fl oz) oven-proof moulds, and pour a tablespoon of golden syrup into each one.

Cream butter and sugar until pale and fluffy. Add eggs one at a time, beating well after each addition. Add milk and stir it in well, then add flour and stir in lightly, until the mixture is quite thick. Spoon the mixture into the pots until three-quarters full, and cover each one with buttered foil. Place in a baking tray of hot water and bake for around 45 minutes until the puddings rise, and spring back to the touch. Remove from oven, and rest for 5 minutes before removing foil and turning out the puddings carefully onto serving plates. Serve hot with pure cream or clotted cream.

Feeds four.

Summer fruit crumble

It's worth waiting for the height of summer to produce this patronisingly simple pud with its rough and crumbly almond topping. The berries will collapse throughout cooking to provide delicious, sticky juices. By all means, put your own mix of fruit together, depending on what's around.

Crumble topping
150 g (5¼ oz) plain flour
½ tsp ground cinnamon
75 g (2½ oz) butter
75 g (2½ oz) brown sugar
2 tbsp ground almonds

2 peaches
2 nectarines
2 apricots
1 green apple
½ mango
1 cup raspberries, blueberries, strawberries
2 tbsp caster sugar

Heat oven to 190°C (375°F). Sift flour and cinnamon into a bowl. Cut butter into tiny cubes and rub lightly into the flour with your fingertips, leaving it clumpy. Mix lightly with sugar and ground almonds.

Peel and roughly chop all fruit as appropriate, and arrange in a jumbled layer in a large buttered pie dish or baking tray. Sprinkle with caster sugar. Top with crumble topping. Bake for 30 to 40 minutes until fruit is hot and topping is golden. Serve hot or warm, with cream, ice cream, or custard.

Feeds four to six.

Sticky toffee pud

This is it – the famous sticky toffee pudding. The original harks back to British boarding schools early this century, and is therefore not my creation. I am merely a disciple, devoted to passing on The Sticky Toffee Word.

180 g (6½ oz) dates, pitted and chopped
1 tsp bicarbonate of soda
1 cup boiling water
50 g (1¾ oz) butter
150 g (5¼ oz) soft brown sugar
2 eggs
180 g (6½ oz) self-raising flour, sifted

Toffee sauce
150 g (5¼ oz) soft brown sugar
250 ml (9 fl oz) light whipping cream
½ tsp vanilla extract
1 tbsp butter

Heat oven to 180°C (350°F). Mix dates and bicarbonate of soda in a heat-proof bowl. Pour boiling water on top and leave to stand.

Cream butter and sugar until pale, then add eggs one at a time, beating well after each addition. Gently fold in the sifted flour, stir in the date mixture, and then pour into a lightly buttered 18 cm (7 in) square or round cake tin. Bake for 30 to 40 minutes, until an inserted skewer comes out clean.

Combine sugar, cream, vanilla extract and butter in a saucepan, bring to the boil, stirring, and simmer for 5 minutes. Set aside until ready to serve, then quickly reheat when needed.

Cut pudding into squares and place each square in the centre of a warm dinner plate. Pour hot toffee sauce over each square, and serve with fresh cream, ice cream or custard.

P.S. Traditionally, the toffee sauce is poured over the cake and returned to the oven for the last 5 minutes of baking to get really sticky. I prefer this slightly less gross method, where sticky sauce meets steamy pudding on the plate.

Feeds four.

Greek rice pudding

Greek *rizogalo* is much loved for its creamy, melting white sweetness. It is often thickened with egg yolks at the end of cooking, but I prefer to keep it on the runny side of firm, thickened only with a little cornflour. Serve it in shallow bowls so you get a maximum amount of area to sprinkle with cinnamon – the best part.

1 litre (1¾ pints) milk
120 g (4¼ oz) short grain or arborio rice
2 tbsp sugar
½ tsp vanilla extract
1 tsp clear rosewater syrup
1 tsp cornflour
1 tsp ground cinnamon

Place milk and rice in a heavy-bottomed saucepan and heat gently, stirring occasionally, while you bring the milk to a simmer. Lower the heat just before the milk comes to the boil and cook gently, uncovered, for 30 to 40 minutes, stirring occasionally, until each grain of rice is tender but still shapely. Add sugar, vanilla and rosewater syrup, and stir well until sugar dissolves.

Mix cornflour to a paste with an extra tablespoon of milk. Add cornflour paste to the rice, raise the heat slightly, and stir well until the mixture thickens to a creamy texture. Pour into 4 shallow individual bowls. Sprinkle with cinnamon and serve warm or cold.

P.S. If you prefer a baked rice pudding with a crusty top, pour the cooked rice into a buttered ovenproof dish, dot with a little butter and bake at 180°C (350°F) for 20 minutes until the top is golden brown.

Feeds four.

Sago pudding

In Malaysia, this popular dessert has taken the name of the palm sugar that sweetens it, *gula melaka*. Look for the small-grained pearl sago in the supermarket. Make your own coconut cream (Pantry, 220), or use the thick, rich 'cream' that has risen to the top of a can of coconut milk.

Syrup
100 g (3½ oz) palm sugar
200 ml (7 fl oz) water

6 cups boiling water
1 cup pearl sago (small grains)
100 ml (3½ fl oz) thick coconut milk from top of can
pinch of salt

Combine palm sugar and water in a small pot and heat, stirring, until sugar has dissolved. Continue simmering until liquid reduces to around three quarters of a cup. Allow to cool.

Bring 6 cups of water to the boil. Add sago in a slow, steady stream, stirring constantly. Cook, stirring, for around 10 to 15 minutes, until sago is soft and transparent. Strain, and rinse under cold running water to wash off excess starch. Drain well.

Mix sago with half the palm sugar syrup, half the coconut milk and salt, and ladle into pour into six 100 ml (3½ fl oz) moulds. Cover and chill for an hour or two.

To serve, unmould sago onto individual serving plates, and top each one with a spoonful of the remaining palm sugar syrup and chilled coconut cream.

Feeds six.

Sticky jam pudding

Use your favourite jam (raspberry is great), or even marmalade, to make this luscious pud, and then more of it to make the berry-pink sauce. Or serve with a home-made custard. Or cream. Or ice cream. Or the lot, depending on just how cold the winter is.

100 g (3½ oz) butter
150 g (5¼ oz) sugar
2 eggs, separated
200 g (7 oz) self-raising flour
pinch salt
2 tbsp milk
1tsp butter
3 tbsp berry jam

Berry sauce
2 tbsp sugar
½ cup whipping cream
2 tbsp berry jam

Beat butter and sugar together until pale and fluffy, and sugar has dissolved. Add egg yolks one after the other, beating well until pale and fluffy. Sift flour and salt into a bowl. Fold sifted flour into egg mixture alternately with milk, until smooth and quite thick. Beat egg whites until snowy, and gently fold into the batter.

Butter a 1 litre (1¾ pint) pudding basin or heat proof bowl. Line the base with buttered greaseproof paper, and smear with the jam. Spoon the batter on top. Cover basin with buttered foil or a tight-fitting lid and place in a steamer on top of the stove, or in a pan half-full of water in a moderate oven. Steam over simmering water for 2 hours, checking water level occasionally in case it boils dry. Remove from steamer, run a knife around the edges to loosen the pudding, and turn out onto a warm platter.

Combine sugar, cream and jam in a saucepan. Heat through, stirring with a wooden spoon until jam has melted. Simmer for 5 minutes, and serve. Pour sauce over the pudding and serve, or cut into wedges and pour sauce on top.

Feeds four to six.

All you need is fresh fruit.

A few ripe berries, a crisp apple, a tangy orange or a juicy pear at the end of the meal, and your mouth is rewarded, your palate refreshed, and your craving fulfilled.

The recipes that follow are gorgeous, but you might just be better off buying a pile of fresh, ripe mangoes, taking a sharp knife, and eating them purely and simply on their own.

Or chilling a few bunches of juicy grapes to serve as ice cubes for the throat.

Or just hanging over the kitchen sink and biting into a fresh peach.

Ah, but wait. Can we leave well enough alone?

Is there something within us that craves the artifice, the vanity, the aching sweetness of dessert?

Or is it textural – do our tongues need creams and custards to know they are tongues?

Innocent pieces of fruit are turned into fools, tarts, jellies and cakes to prove the validity of our existence.

(I hate to think what banana custard says about us.)

Our love of sweet things must be more than just a mindless nostalgia for the treats of our childhood, a return to innocence and a time before gun laws and cybercrimes.

We're over that.

This is human nature meeting mother nature; an acknowledgement of the need for goodness, truth and beauty in our lives.

There is poetry in a wobbly milk jelly that tastes of almonds and smells of blossom,

and a hint of the divine in a chilled, wine-soaked peach.

But it must be said.

If you are bored with fresh fruit, you are bored with life,

and no recipe for drunken peaches, or panettone with berries, or even rich chocolate mousse,

is going to save you.

Sweets

Ancient Roman baked custard
Watermelon salad
Almond milk jelly
Snow eggs with toffee
Rich chocolate mousse
Panettone with berries
Crêpes with lemon sugar
Crème caramel
Affogato
Thai fruit salad with chilli
Pavlova with passionfruit curd
Drunken peaches

Ancient Roman baked custard

Just when you think civilisation has done a reasonable job of advancing itself, you discover a simple recipe known as *tyropatinum*, recorded by Apicius in *De Re Coquinaria* roughly two thousand years ago, that is pretty similar to the baked custard you pulled out of the oven last Sunday night. Sigh. The pepper is a surprise, but it works.

500 ml (18 fl oz) milk
100 ml (3½ fl oz) wild honey
5 eggs, beaten
freshly ground pepper

Heat oven to 160°C (325°F). Heat milk and honey in a saucepan, stirring, without allowing to boil. Cool milk for 10 minutes. Place beaten eggs in a large bowl and slowly pour in milk and honey, whisking until well mixed.

Strain mixture into a heat-proof glass or earthenware baking dish and place in a roasting tray or baking pan. Fill pan with water until the level reaches half way up the side of the dish. Bake for 30 to 40 minutes or until just set. Grind black pepper on top, and serve.

Feeds four.

Watermelon salad

They look like precious, delicate sorbets. They even taste like them. On the hottest, longest, stickiest day of summer, go out early in the morning and buy a variety of ripe melons. Chill them all day and by the time the sun goes down, you will have an instant smorgasbord of refreshments that even come with their own edible plates.

1 red-fleshed watermelon
1 yellow-fleshed (champagne) melon
1 honeydew melon

Keep melons as chilled as possible.

Cut four 2.5 cm (1 in) thick round slices from the middle of the watermelon to serve as plates. Use a large ice-cream scoop to scoop out balls of watermelon flesh from the ends.

Cut champagne and honeydew melons in half and scoop out balls of the flesh.

Arrange melon balls on melon plates. Resist the temptation to do any more than this.

Feeds four to six.

Almond milk jelly

A shivering, shimmering jelly that looks innocently pure and white, and tastes angelically of almonds. Made throughout the Middle East for centuries, this could be its lightest and purest incarnation yet.

200 g (7 oz) blanched almonds
500 ml (18 fl oz) milk
100 grams (3½ oz) caster sugar
200 ml (7 fl oz) water
10 g (¼ oz) powdered gelatine
almond oil for moulds

Grind or blend almonds to a paste. Heat milk to just below boiling point, add almonds and leave to infuse until cool, stirring occasionally.

Bring caster sugar and water to the boil in a small saucepan, stirring until sugar has dissolved. Remove from heat, add gelatine, and stir until dissolved. Leave gelatine mixture to cool, stirring occasionally.

Pour almond milk through a layer of dampened muslin, squeezing to extract the juices, until you have 300 ml (10 fl oz). Discard ground almonds. Combine the gelatine mixture and 300 ml almond milk, stirring carefully. Chill for 10 minutes and stir again.

Divide the mixture between six 100 ml moulds, very lightly oiled with almond oil. Chill in refrigerator overnight, or at least for a few hours.

Turn out moulds and serve with freshly poached peaches, cherries or plums.

Feeds six.

Snow eggs with toffee

Known throughout French bistros as *oeufs à la neige* because they look like eggs of snow resting on a lake of golden custard. The cleverness, however, is in the kitchen, as the egg yolks that are not used in the mousse are used in the custard, in one of those great, lasting examples of good housewifery.

Snow eggs
6 egg whites
100 g (3½ oz) caster sugar
½ tsp vanilla essence

Custard
500 ml (18 fl oz) milk
1 split vanilla bean
6 egg yolks
85 g (3 oz) caster sugar

Caramel
5 tbsp sugar
water to cover

Bring the milk to the boil in a shallow pan, then reduce to a gentle simmer. Beat egg whites and salt until firm and peaky, then beat in sugar and vanilla extract until mixture is glossy and firm.

Use a large spoon to shape a 'football' of meringue and slip it onto the milk. Poach four meringues at a time for two minutes, then turn to poach the other side for another one or two minutes. Remove meringues with a slotted spoon and drain on absorbent paper. Cook remaining meringues, then strain the milk into a saucepan.

Whisk or beat egg yolks and sugar together for a few minutes until the mixture forms ribbons that fall from the whisk. Pour milk gradually into the egg mixture, whisking slowly until combined. Return to saucepan and cook very gently, stirring constantly with a wooden spoon for 10 to 15 minutes, until custard thickens. Strain into a bowl and allow to cool, stirring occasionally. Divide custard among four shallow pasta bowls and top each with a meringue.

Melt sugar for caramel in a small saucepan with just enough water to cover, stirring until it bubbles. Stop stirring, and watch carefully as water evaporates and caramel turns golden. Use the prongs of a fork to drizzle the caramel carefully over each meringue.

Feeds four.

Rich chocolate mousse

Not your pale and fluffy imitation, but the real thing, made of nothing but chocolate and fresh eggs, and a little cognac. It sets quite firmly, but melts in the mouth like rich chocolate ice cream. For a massive chocolate attack, double the recipe and serve in a huge white pot at the table, with one giant spoon.

200 g (7 oz) chocolate couverture
6 free range eggs
1 tbsp cognac, Armagnac or rum

Break or chop chocolate into small pieces and place in a large heat-proof bowl standing over a pan of simmering water. Stir occasionally with a wooden spoon while chocolate melts.

Separate eggs, placing yolks in one large bowl, and whites in another. Beat egg yolks until well mixed. Remove chocolate from heat, allow to cool slightly, then pour into egg yolks while beating. Add cognac, mixing well:

Whisk the egg whites until stiff and softly peaky, but not too dry. Add a large spoonful of egg whites to the chocolate mixture and mix well, then gently fold in the remaining egg white. Pour mixture into a serving bowl.

Chill for an hour or two until set.

Feeds four.

Panettone with berries

The plump, round, dome-shaped panettone of light, golden brioche is one of Italy's most delicious creations. Romance has it that in the fifteenth century, the beautiful daughter of a Milanese baker called Toni attracted a young aristocrat, who soon became the baker's new apprentice. Used to fancier fare, the newcomer enriched the bread of Toni (pan di Toni) with fruit and citron peel, making it a household name. Make sure your panettone is neither iced nor chocolate-coated, or things could get messy.

1 plain or fruit panettone
3 punnets of mixed summer berries
1 tbsp fresh mint leaves
3 tbsp berry liqueur e.g. Framboise, Crême de Cassis
2 tbsp soft brown sugar
400 ml (14 fl oz) cream or natural yoghurt
icing sugar

Slice the panettone into four equal plate-size rounds. Wash and dry the berries. Hull any strawberries, but leave any red currants on their stems.

Combine berries, mint, liqueur and sugar in a saucepan. Heat very gently until berries are warm and starting to exude their own juices, and sugar is dissolved.

Heat the grill and lightly toast the panettone rounds on both sides. Arrange panettone on four plates and spoon berries and juices on top. Dust with icing sugar. Serve with a big bowl of natural yoghurt or cream.

Feeds four.

Crêpes with lemon sugar

The sharp fruity bite of lemon juice, the crackling texture of sugar, and the smooth, rich butteriness of paper-thin crêpes – it's a classic. Eating these crêpes is a bit like waking up in bed to find you are nibbling your satin sheets.

100 g (3½ oz) plain flour
40 g (1½ oz) caster sugar
pinch of salt
1 egg
1 egg yolk
200 ml (7 fl oz) milk
1 tbsp butter
extra butter for pan
2 extra tbsp caster sugar
grated rind of 1 lemon
juice of 2 lemons

Blend flour, sugar, salt, whole egg and egg yolk in food processor. Add milk gradually, with the motor running, until mixture is smooth and creamy. Melt the butter in a small saucepan until foaming and golden. Add melted butter to crêpe batter and blend for 10 seconds. Rest batter for at least 30 minutes.

Brush the crêpe pan with melted butter, over medium heat. Add a ladleful of batter and swirl the pan so it covers the base thinly. Cook for a minute or two until base is lightly golden and crisped at the edges. Turn the crêpe over and cook other side very briefly. Slide out the crêpe and repeat process with remaining batter. Keep crêpes warm in a low oven while finishing the rest.

Mix sugar and grated lemon rind. Sprinkle each crêpe with sugar mixture and lemon juice. Fold in half, then half again, or roll into tight cylinders. Sprinkle with more lemon juice and sugar and serve with vanilla bean ice cream.

Makes six.

Crème caramel

There is a very good reason why crème caramel has become so damnably clichéd. It's delicious. I often infuse the milk with lemon rind for extra fragrance and a light citrusy accent, but otherwise, there's not much I would want to change.

1 litre (1¾ pints) milk
6 tbsp caster sugar
rind of one lemon
1 vanilla bean, split lengthwise
6 eggs
3 extra egg yolks

Caramel
6 tbsp caster sugar
water to cover (just)

Combine milk, sugar, lemon rind and vanilla bean and bring slowly to the boil. Remove from heat and leave to stand for 1 hour to infuse.

Heat the sugar for the caramel with just enough water to cover, stirring, until bubbles appear. Stop stirring and continue to cook, watching carefully, as water evaporates and liquid starts turning golden brown. Remove from heat immediately and pour carefully into a 20 cm (8 in) mould or cake tin, or 8 individual moulds, swirling to coat the sides and bottom. Set coated moulds aside.

Mix eggs and extra yolks lightly, in a bowl. Strain cooled milk into egg mixture, whisking. Strain again, into the caramelised baking dish.

Cover with foil and place in a roasting pan half-filled with hot water. Cook at 180°C (350°F) for 30 to 40 minutes (one large mould) or 20 to 30 minutes (small moulds) or until set. Allow to cool, and store in refrigerator for at least 6 hours.

Run a knife around the edge, place a large platter on top, and quickly invert the plate to unmould onto platter, allowing caramel to flow gently down the sides.

Feeds four to eight.

Affogato

Further proof that cooking is alchemy. A great magic happens when hot espresso coffee is poured over icy cold ice cream in this Italian creation, literally meaning 'drowned'. Look for the tell-tale flecks of vanilla bean in your ice cream to prove its quality, or buy the finest coffee-flavoured ice cream for an extra hit of caffeine.

4 or 8 scoops of vanilla bean ice cream
300 ml (10 fl oz) hot espresso coffee
8 tbsp chilled cognac or liqueur

Drop scoops of vanilla bean ice cream into four chilled parfait or cocktail glasses. Pour 4 shot glasses of chilled Cognac or your favourite liqueur (I love Nocello or Frangelico). Make 4 small cups of very hot espresso coffee.

Place 1 glass of ice cream, 1 glass of liqueur, and 1 espresso cup on each serving plate or small tray.

Invite quests to pour first the coffee, then the liqueur over the ice cream, and eat it with a spoon while it melts into a dreamy, creamy mess.

Feeds four.

Thai fruit salad with chilli

Somehow a little bit of chilli will sneak into just about everything in Thailand, even a snack of fresh fruit. This tropical fruit salad is given a velvet-booted kick with a sweet syrup infused with ginger and chilli.

200 g (7 oz) white sugar
1 cup water
1 tbsp grated ginger
1 small red chilli, sliced
juice of one lime
1 lime, sliced
1 small bunch mint
800 g (1¾ lb) your choice of cherries, grapes,
    mangoes, stone fruit, strawberries, rambutan, lychees,
    melons, nectarine, paw paw, pineapple, cut and
    trimmed as appropriate
1 extra lime
1 extra red chilli

Dissolve sugar in water over gentle heat. Add ginger, chilli, lime, lime juice, and half the mint leaves and bring to the boil. Allow to bubble until it starts to turn a light golden colour and reduces in volume slightly. Cool and strain.

Toss fresh fruit pieces with remaining fresh mint leaves in the syrup and pile high on a platter or inside a glass bowl. Top with extra slices of lime, and an extra fresh chilli if you're feeling racy.

Feeds four.

Pavlova with passionfruit curd

History and rumour have it that the pavlova was created in Australia in 1935 by a Perth hotel chef called Bert Sachse, and was named after the great ballerina Anna Pavlova, who had successfully performed there a few years earlier. But history and rumour can be challenged, and there is reason to believe that meringue cakes of a similar style were common in New Zealand years earlier. I like to make mine in free-range blobs rather than neat, suburban rings.

Meringue
6 egg whites
200 g (7 oz) caster sugar
½ tsp vanilla extract
1 tsp vinegar
1 tsp boiling water

Cream
1 cup thickened cream
½ cup natural yoghurt
1 cup passionfruit curd (Pantry, 220)
  or 6 tbsp passionfruit pulp

Heat oven to 120°C (250°F).

Beat egg whites in a clean dry bowl until firm. Add sugar and beat strongly for 5 good minutes. Add vanilla extract, water, and vinegar and fold through egg whites.

Plop six large spoonfuls of meringue onto a baking tray covered with baking paper. Bake for 1 hour until crisp but still pale on the outside, and a bit soft and marshmallowy inside. Turn off oven and leave meringues to cool in the oven for a further hour.

Store in an airtight jar or tin until needed. Beat cream until thick and ploppy, and stir in yoghurt.

Top each meringue with a spoonful of yoghurt cream, and a spoonful of passionfruit curd, or passionfruit pulp, and serve.

Feeds six.

Drunken peaches

This is the next best thing to leaning over the sink eating ripe, juicy, dribbly peaches on their own. Serve each rose-coloured peach in the middle of a white shallow bowl, like a pasta bowl, so that everyone can still lean forward and dribble.

750 ml (26 fl oz) rosé
200 g (7 oz) caster sugar
2 cinnamon sticks, broken in half
6 peaches
6 amaretti biscuits

Combine wine, sugar and cinnamon sticks in a saucepan, and bring to the boil. Simmer until it no longer smells alcoholic, or until slightly reduced in volume, around 10 minutes. Allow to cool.

Peel peaches by lightly cutting the skin from top to bottom and immersing in a pot of simmering water for 5 seconds. Dunk into a bowl of cold water and peel off skin. Arrange peaches snugly in a high-sided glass dish. Top with rosé, and chill for 3 hours. Turn peaches 2 or 3 times during the 3 hours, as they take on the colour of the wine.

Serve each person one peach, very chilled, with a few spoonfuls of rosé around it. Crush amaretti biscuits into crumbs and scatter on top of each peach.

P.S. On a really, really hot day, just pour the rosé over the peeled peaches and chill well before serving. It is totally refreshing because the only sweetness comes from the fruit itself.

Feeds six.

Nobody can teach you how to make the perfect cup of tea. It just happens, over time.

Wearing cashmere helps, of course.

As does ignoring the old maxim of one for each person and one for the pot, which is too strong for a fine quality leaf.

Fresh water is vital: collect rain water for your tea, and taste the difference.

Try blending your own tea from different leaves, and serving them at different times of the day.

And please, do not automatically offer Earl Grey. There are far too many of us who hate it.

Herbal tea is often a happy alternative: just don't give chamomile tea to a person who is already boring.

Coffee is a perfectly acceptable beverage at afternoon tea. It's just that 'come to afternoon coffee' has no resonance.

It is also important to have afternoon tea by yourself as you would wish to be seen having afternoon tea if someone arrived unexpectedly in the middle of it.

A good afternoon tea is wittier than a cocktail party and more socially satisfying than a dinner party.

My grandmother's advice was to always have something savoury –

some tiny ham sandwiches, baby sausages wrapped in warm pastry – for the men.

But it's the cake that is the heart and soul of afternoon tea, the architectural monument that bonds people,

pulling them to the table and to the tea-pot.

Please avoid the use of all words such as wicked, naughty and sinful when thinking about, cooking, serving and eating cake. They are completely irrelevant.

The correct words are well deserved, essential and invaluable.

As for people who offer you tea or coffee without anything scrumptious to eat, Winnie The Pooh's advice is,

as always, sensible.

'When you're visiting a friend and you find that it is time for a little smackerel of something,

try looking wistfully in the direction of the cupboard.'

Afternoon Tea

Sachertorte
Anzac biscuits
Risotto cake
Rich chocolate brownies
Date and walnut loaf
Almond biscotti
German plum cake
Chocolate espresso cake
Chocolate chip cookies
Gingerbread
Lemon cheese cake
Boil and bake fruit cake

Sachertorte

My interpretation (easier, faster, no return airfare) of the famous cake from the Hotel Sacher in Vienna, lined with apricot jam and enrobed with chocolate. Make sure you beat the egg yolks and sugar well, and don't overfold the flour into the final mixture.

6 eggs (65 g), separated
180 g (6½ oz) sugar
½ tsp vanilla extract
150 g (5¼ oz) plain flour
4 tbsp bitter (unsweetened) cocoa powder
butter for cake tin
150 g (5¼ oz) apricot jam
100 g (3½ oz) bitter chocolate or couverture
100 g (3½ oz) butter, chopped

Heat oven to 180°C (350°F). Butter a 23 cm (9 in) diameter spring-form cake tin. Sift flour and cocoa powder together into a bowl and set aside.

Beat egg yolks and sugar until so thick and creamy it forms ribbons when you lift the beater. Stir in vanilla extract.

Beat the egg whites until stiff and peaky. Fold a little egg white into the egg yolk mixture, then the remaining egg whites. Fold the sifted flour and cocoa powder into the mixture, 2 tablespoonsful at a time. Transfer the quite thick mixture into the cake tin and bake for 30 to 35 minutes until a thin skewer inserted in the centre comes out dry. Cool in tin for 10 minutes, then remove from tin and cool completely.

Cut cake into 2 equal rounds and trim the top of the cake to be level, if you like. Place the cake base on a wire rack over a baking tin to catch drips. Warm apricot jam with a little water and spread a thin layer on the top of the bottom half. Replace top half of the cake and spread top and sides with apricot jam.

Melt chocolate and butter in a heat-proof bowl set over a saucepan of simmering water, stirring, until smooth and glossy. Pour chocolate over the top of the cake and sides, smoothing the sides with a hot palette knife if necessary. Chill for an hour or two before serving, until icing has set.

Feeds six to eight.

Anzac biscuits

I used to think these biscuits were named after my father, who was born in 1916, soon after the landing of the Australian and New Zealand Army Corps (ANZAC) at Gallipoli in 1915, and christened Edward Anzac as a result. In fact, these sweet and crunchy biscuits are old Australian favourites named in honour of the ANZAC soldiers, as he was.

100 g (3½ oz) rolled oats
60 g (2 oz) desiccated coconut
175 g (6 oz) plain all-purpose flour, sifted
125 g (4½ oz) soft brown sugar
125 g (4½ oz) butter
3 tbsp boiling water
2 tbsp golden syrup
1 tsp bicarbonate of soda

Mix oats, coconut, flour and sugar in a large bowl.

Butter 2 baking trays and heat oven to 150°C (300°F). Heat butter, water and golden syrup in a saucepan, stirring, until butter melts. Remove from heat and quickly stir in bicarbonate of soda until light and frothy.

Pour the mixture into the dry ingredients, mixing quickly and thoroughly. Roll mixture into balls the size of walnuts and place on trays, allowing room for spreading.

Press down gently with a spatula, and bake for 20 minutes until lightly golden and still slightly soft. Remove trays from oven and leave biscuits to cool on the trays for 10 minutes. Transfer to wire racks to cool completely until crisp on the outside, but still a little chewy inside.

Store in an airtight jar as soon as biscuits have cooled.

Makes twenty-five.

Risotto cake

Virtually a delicious rice pudding in the form of a cake, scented with lemon rind and flavoured with ground almonds and candied peel. Serve as a cake or as a dessert, warm or at room temperature.

1 litre (1¾ pints) milk
1 cup sugar
grated rind of 1 lemon
1 cup arborio rice
5 eggs
3 tbsp ground almonds
3 tbsp candied peel
2 tbsp rum
2 tbsp icing sugar

Combine milk, sugar and lemon rind in a saucepan and bring to the boil. Add rice and simmer gently, uncovered, for 40 to 50 minutes or until the rice has absorbed all the milk. (Depending on your rice, you may need to add another half-cup of milk). Remove from heat, cover, and allow to cool.

Heat the oven to 180°C (350° F). Oil a 25 cm (10 in) cake pan with removable base.

Beat eggs well, in a large bowl. Add cooled rice, ground almonds, mixed peel and rum and stir well. Pour into pan and bake for 1 hour or until cooked. Test cake by piercing it with a thin skewer – if it comes out dry, not wet, the cake is cooked.

Serve with poached fruits and cream while still warm, or cool to room temperature, dust with sifted icing sugar and cut into wedges.

Feeds eight.

Rich chocolate brownies

A full-on hit of rich, dense, gooey pure chocolate brownies, cooked in a slab and cut into generous, messy, fudgy squares. It will keep cooking as it cools in the tin, and the top will sink, crack and look like a disaster area. This is good.

250 g (9 oz) dark bitter chocolate, chopped
175 g (6 oz) butter
175 g (6 oz) white sugar
3 eggs (65 g)
½ tsp vanilla extract
100 g (3½ oz) walnuts, roughly chopped
100 g (3½ oz) plain flour
1 level tsp baking powder

Heat oven to 180°C (350°F).

Butter a cake tin or baking tray measuring 25 cm by 30 cm (10 in by 12 in). Melt chocolate and butter in a heat-proof bowl set over a pot of gently simmering water, stirring occasionally. Remove from the heat, and allow to cool for 10 minutes.

Beat sugar and eggs in a large bowl until pale and creamy. Fold chocolate mixture into egg mixture. Add vanilla extract and walnuts, and stir well. Sift in flour and baking powder, and fold gently until just mixed. Pour mixture into tin.

Bake for 30 to 35 minutes, or until a skewer inserted in centre comes out moist but not wet. Allow to cool in tin, then cut into squares and remove from tin. Pile high to serve and dust with icing sugar.

Makes twelve squares.

Date and walnut loaf

Dig out that old tube cake tin your grandmother left you and don't let this incredibly easy, wonderfully moist, deliciously sweet favourite die out. If you don't have a tube tin, or you can't find the lids for both ends (a common problem), use a 25 cm by 10 cm (10 in by 4 in) loaf tin. If you don't have a ripe banana, add a tablespoon of golden syrup for extra moistness.

150 g (5¼ oz) dates, chopped
100 g (3½ oz) brown sugar
50 g (1¾ oz) chopped walnuts
1 small ripe banana, cut into small chunks
1 tbsp butter
1 tsp bicarbonate of soda
1 cup boiling water
200 g (7 oz) self-raising flour, sifted

Heat oven to 190°C (375°F).

Butter a 20 cm by 10 cm (8 in by 4 in) tube tin and its two lids. Butter 2 squares of greaseproof paper for the lids.

Combine dates, sugar, walnuts, banana, butter, bicarbonate of soda and boiling water in a bowl. Mix well, and leave to cool. Add sifted flour and mix well.

Cover one end of the tube tin with a square of buttered greaseproof paper, and jam on the lid. Place lid side down and fill tin to two-thirds with batter. Cover top end of tin with remaining square of greaseproof paper and jam on the lid. Lie tin on its side in a baking tray and bake for 1 hour.

Remove from oven and leave for 1 hour to cool. Run a knife between cake and tin, and gently ease out the cake. Leave on wire cake rack to cool.

Feeds four to six.

Almond biscotti

The first baking gives you fragrant loaves of Italian almond bread. The second baking gives you teeth-achingly crisp, dry-as-bones *cantucci di Prato*. Serve with an espresso coffee, a glass of Vin Santo or your favourite Italian liqueur for dunking.

100 g (3½ oz) almonds
250 g (9 oz) plain flour
1 tsp baking powder
240 g (8½ oz) caster sugar
½ tsp vanilla extract
2 eggs
1 extra egg yolk

Heat oven to 180°C (350°F). Toast almonds in a hot, dry pan until they smell sweet and nutty, then cool and roughly chop.

Combine flour, baking powder, sugar, vanilla extract, whole eggs and egg yolk in a food processor and blend until the mixture leaves the sides and forms a ball.

Turn out onto a lightly floured bench and sprinkle with the almonds. Knead for a minute or two to mix them through. Divide dough in 2 and pat out into log shapes about 25 cm long and 5 cm wide (10 in by 2 in).

Lightly butter a baking tray and arrange logs with room for spreading to the side. Bake for 30 to 35 minutes until they are lightly coloured and firm to the touch. Remove tray and allow biscotti to cool for 10 or 15 minutes, while you reduce the oven temperature to 140°C (275°F).

Cut the logs on the diagonal, into 1 cm (½ in) slices or slightly thicker if you like. Arrange on a tray and return to the oven for about 20 to 30 minutes until quite dry, without allowing them to colour. Remove tray and allow to cool on tray until cold, when they will be crisp and dry.

Store in an airtight container.

Makes around forty.

German plum cake

The current chatelaines of Acland Street's famous Monarch cake shop in Melbourne have very kindly passed on this recipe for my favourite German/Jewish plum cake, baked at the Monarch every day since it opened in the early 1930s. Serve warm from the oven as a fruit pudding or at room temperature as a cake.

200 g (7 oz) butter
160 g (5 oz) sugar
4 eggs (70 g)
½ tsp vanilla extract
100 g (3½ oz) plain flour
125 g (4½ oz) self-raising flour
pinch of salt
12 blood plums or 20 apricots
2 tbsp icing sugar

Heat oven to 180°C (350°F). Butter and paper a baking tray or pie dish measuring 30 cm by 20 cm (12 in by 8 in), or a 30 cm (12 in) diameter springform baking tin.

Cream butter and sugar together until pale and creamy. Add eggs, one at a time, beating well after each addition. Stir in vanilla extract. Sift both flours and salt together. Beat flour into batter until well mixed. Cut plums or apricots around their circumference, twist apart and remove stones. Arrange fruit, cut side up, in neat rows on top of batter.

Bake for 30 to 40 minutes, until a thin skewer inserted in the centre comes out clean. Remove from oven and dust with icing sugar through a fine sieve. Serve warm or cold straight from the pan, cutting across into slices.

Or dust with extra icing sugar and serve with fresh cream.

Makes around sixteen slices.

Chocolate espresso cake

I swear I will put this classic French flourless chocolate, coffee and almond cake in every cook book I ever do, just in case there is one person out there who doesn't already know it. I first came across it in Elizabeth David's *French Provincial Cooking*, immediately doubled the chocolate content and have been pathetically grateful ever since.

200 g (7 oz) dark, bitter chocolate (couverture), chopped
1 tbsp strong espresso coffee
1 tbsp rum or brandy
150 g (5¼ oz) caster sugar
150 g (5¼ oz) butter
100 g (3½ oz) ground almonds or hazelnuts
5 eggs, separated
icing sugar for dusting

Heat oven to 180°C (350°F). Melt the chocolate, coffee, rum or brandy, sugar and butter in a bowl sitting in a pot of simmering water. Remove from heat and stir until well mixed.

Add ground almonds and mix well. Beat in the egg yolks, one by one. Beat egg whites until stiff and peaky, and stir a couple of spoonfuls into the chocolate mixture to lighten it, before gently folding in the rest.

Turn into a buttered and floured 20 cm (8 in) round or square cake tin, and bake for 40 to 50 minutes. Leave to cool before removing from tin and don't worry if the crust falls and collapses. That's perfectly normal, if not desirable. Dust with icing sugar to serve.

Feeds six.

Chocolate chip cookies

Fannie Farmer's 1896 *Cook Book* lists a recipe for a German chocolate cookie flavoured with pieces of chocolate. This evolved into the famous Tollhouse chocolate chip cookie with a little help from Ruth Wakefield of the Toll House Inn in Massachusetts in the 1930s. She then sold the rights to the Tollhouse cookie name to the Nestlé company, so we are left with calling them chocolate chip cookies. Which is what they are anyway.

125 g (4½ oz) butter
125 g (4½ oz) white sugar
125 g (4½ oz) brown sugar
2 eggs, beaten
250 g (9 oz) self-raising flour, sifted
1 tsp baking powder
½ tsp salt
1 cup dark chocolate or semi-sweet chocolate chips
1 cup walnuts or almonds, finely chopped
1 tsp vanilla extract

Heat oven to 190°C (375°F). Whizz butter with both sugars in food processor. Add beaten eggs, sifted flour, baking powder and salt and whizz again. Chop dark chocolate (if using) into little chunks. Stir chocolate and nuts and vanilla into mixture. Plop spoonfuls of mixture onto a nonstick baking tray, allowing room to grow.

Bake for 10 to 15 minutes until lightly golden. Cool on a wire rack and store in an airtight container.

Makes twelve.

Gingerbread

Gingerbread has been munched in France since the eleventh century, when the Gingerbread Fair was first held in Paris. The local monks would sell their own gingerbread, shaped into little pigs. This may have been what gave the first Queen Elizabeth the idea of ordering little ginger cakes (the first gingerbread men) to be baked in the shapes of portraits of those she knew. You might like to pursue the same idea.

115 g (4 oz) soft brown sugar
175 ml (5½ fl oz) golden syrup
90 g (3¼ oz) butter
1 tbsp ground ginger
1 tbsp ground cinnamon
1 tsp fresh grated ginger
1 tbsp bicarbonate of soda
500 g (1 lb) plain flour
pinch of salt
2 eggs, beaten

Combine sugar, golden syrup, butter, spices and fresh ginger in a heavy-based pan over low heat, and let melt, stirring. Remove from heat and cool for 2 minutes, then quickly stir in bicarbonate of soda until light and fluffy.

Sift flour and salt into a large mixing bowl. Make a well in the centre, add eggs and gradually add the syrup, stirring until all flour is incorporated and you have a dough. Wrap dough in plastic and chill for 1 hour.

Heat oven to 180°C (350°F) and roll out dough thinly on a floured surface. Cut into the shapes of men, women, animals, stars, trees or rounds, and place on trays lined with baking paper. Bake for 10 minutes. Remove from oven and let cool for 5 minutes before removing from tray. Cool on wire rack, and store in airtight container.

Makes about twenty-five biscuits, or twelve men and women.

Lemon cheese cake

There are cheese cakes and there are cheese cakes, but this – now *this* – is a real cheese cake, a baked, rich, lightly golden, lemon scented creamy tart in true central European style. I prefer to serve on the day it is baked without chilling it, which seems to deaden the flavour. Serve with poached cherries, plums, berries or passionfruit curd for a glam dessert.

200 g (7 oz) caster sugar
3 eggs (65 g)
750 g (1½ lb) soft cream cheese
300 ml (10 fl oz) sour cream
1 tbsp lemon juice
1 tsp vanilla extract
2 level tbsp custard powder sifted

Heat oven to 180°C (350°F). Beat sugar and eggs together until smooth, using a hand-held or electric mixer. Add cream cheese and sour cream gradually, beating until smooth for up to 10 minutes.

Stir in lemon juice and vanilla extract, and mix in sifted custard powder. Pour into a lightly buttered 22 cm (8½ in) diameter springform cake tin and smooth the mixture evenly.

Bake for 50 to 60 minutes until the centre is firm, and the top is lightly golden and looks as if it is just about to split. Turn off the oven, leave the door ajar and leave the cake in the oven to cool completely.

Slice into wedges to serve on the same day, or chill if serving the next day.

Feeds six.

Boil and bake fruit cake

An easy old thing from Ireland that would have been as popular a few hundred years ago as it is now, for its household economy, simplicity and exceptional keeping qualities. This is also a great recipe with which to launch kids into the kitchen, setting them on the path of self-reliance, kitchen confidence and cake adoration by virtue of their first, delicious success.

150 g (5¼ oz) butter
300 g (11 oz) sultanas
300 g (11 oz) currants
180 g (6½ oz) soft brown sugar
1 tsp ground allspice
1 tsp ground cinnamon
1 tsp ground ginger
1 tsp bicarbonate of soda
1 cup water
2 eggs, well beaten
150 g (5¼ oz) plain flour
150 g (5¼ oz) self-raising flour

Heat oven to 180°C (350°F).

Combine butter, sultanas, currants, sugar, allspice, cinnamon, ginger, bicarbonate of soda and water in a saucepan. Bring to the boil, stirring, then cool.

Add eggs and beat well. Sift the 2 flours together, add to the mixture and beat well. Pour into a lightly buttered cake tin of 22 cm (8½ in) diameter. Bake for 1 hour or until a skewer inserted in centre comes out clean.

Remove from oven and allow to cool slightly before removing from tin. Store in an airtight container.

Feeds six.

Opera, film, evening classes and drinks after work were only invented because we love supper so much.

We love that aren't-I-naughty staying up late feeling,

that genuine hunger emanating from the hole where our stomachs used to be,

that need for something warm, delicious and fast that lies like a hotpot of gold at the end of our cultural rainbow.

Of course, by this time, we are so hungry, we will swallow anything as long as it has cheese on it.

So think soup, risotto, pasta, little cheesy toasty things, warm salads, and luxurious foods like salmon.

Chinese rice congee is one of the world's most adored suppers, but its bland innocence is an acquired taste for those who didn't acquire it during a Chinese childhood.

Creamy scrambled eggs strewn with fresh herbs are fast to cook and slow to eat, and can be teamed with luscious smoked salmon and grilled sourdough bread.

The word supper comes from the French term *souper*, to take soup, and was once the only evening meal.

Then it became an intimate late dinner in high society, and still it conjures up images of opera boxes, gleaming silver, sparkling wine, and rich, blonde food like oysters in cream.

But we need food our stomachs can cope with late at night – vegetables, rice, soups, and fish, light on oil and animal fats.

Suppers should be, by their very nature, unpretentious.

Remember the sort of stuff you ate when you finally reached home after school, utterly convinced you were starving to death? That's what makes a good supper.

A mug of pea soup, a platter of bread and ripe tomatoes, or a large piece of a wonderful cake.

No showing off with expensive, rare and indigestible ingredients;

no formally set tables and legions of wine glasses banked before you;

no interminable *hors d'oeuvres* and *amuse-gueules* and other excuses for putting off getting stuck into some decent food.

Just big bowls and platters of things you can eat with a fork or a spoon,

bread you can tear with your hands, salad you can pick up with your fingers,

and wine you can pour down your throat as if there were no tomorrow.

A quick herb omelette or a platter of steamed asparagus garnished with grated Parmigiano cheese and you have a memorable meal worth staying up for.

Mushrooms on toast can be elegant if the mushrooms are tossed with fresh herbs and served on grilled brioche.

A gentle soufflé makes a sophisticated supper, especially when made with a great gruyère cheese.

And never forget the power of leftovers to live two lives.

It is worth poaching a huge corner of corned beef (silverside) for dinner one night,

so that you can make a quick corned beef hash for supper the following night.

If you make a mountain of mashed potato one day, you can turn it into gnocchi the next.

Last night's risotto can be shaped into balls, rolled in breadcrumbs and fried.

Cooked jasmine rice can be spread out to dry during the day and turned into fresh-as-a-daisy fried rice when you get home after whatever it is that took you out.

And never underestimate the power of bread and cheese.

At the very least, sandwich slices of good cheese and ham between two slices of plain white bread,

so that all you have to do is butter them on the outside and let them cook slowly in a frypan over low heat, turning once,

until golden brown and as crisp as a potato chip on the outside, and meltingly soft inside.

Divine.

Supper

Broken pasta
Ma po beancurd
Goat's cheese bruschetta
Fish steak sandwich
Salmon fish cakes
Marmitako
Salt cod with creamed leeks
Risi e bisi
Soba noodles with salmon
Mozza in carrozza
Meat loaf
Pipérade

Broken pasta

This old southern Italian recipe is the only pasta dish I know that is cooked *with* its sauce in the same pan. The pasta absorbs the tomato sauce as it cooks, giving it an extraordinary texture and taste.

3 tbsp olive oil
1 onion, finely chopped
400 g (14 oz) spaghettini, linguini or any very thin pasta
500 g (1 lb) canned roma tomatoes, undrained
2 tbsp black olives, stoned and chopped
½ fresh red chilli, finely chopped
2 tbsp capers, rinsed
½ cup dry white wine
500 ml (18 fl oz) of water
sea salt and freshly ground black pepper
1 tbsp finely chopped Italian parsley
Parmigiano for grating

Heat oil in a large shallow frying pan, and cook onion until soft. Break pasta in half lengthwise, and add to pan.

Add tomatoes, olives, chilli and capers and stir with a wooden spoon until well mixed. Cover the pan and simmer very gently for 3 minutes.

Remove cover, raise heat and add the wine, stirring well so that the pasta doesn't stick to the bottom of the pan. Keep cooking, adding water as needed and stirring constantly for around 20 minutes or until pasta is al dente, tender but still firm to the bite. Add sea salt, pepper and parsley and stir well. Divide among warmed pasta plates and serve with freshly grated Parmigiano.

Feeds four.

Ma po beancurd

A pock-marked grandmother from Chengdu in the peppery province of Sichuan came up with this now-famous dish, a fiery stir-fry of beancurd and pork sauce. Restaurants tend to make this a dish of pork garnished with beancurd, but I prefer to return it to its original intent: a dish of beancurd garnished with pork. Serve wth plenty of rice and a spicy Shiraz.

6 blocks fresh beancurd
1 tbsp peanut oil
1 garlic clove, crushed
1 red chilli, sliced
1 tsp grated ginger
250 g (9 oz) minced pork
3 green (spring) onions, finely chopped
2 tbsp chilli bean sauce
½ tsp sugar
1 tbsp rice wine or dry sherry
2 tbsp dark soy sauce
½ tsp Sichuan peppercorns (fagara), ground
125 ml (4 fl oz) chicken broth
6 sprigs coriander

Cut beancurd blocks into 2 cm (¾ in) cubes, and set aside to drain for 15 minutes.

Heat wok, add oil, and heat. When hot, add garlic, chilli and ginger. Add minced pork and stir fry for 5 minutes. Add green onions, chilli bean sauce, sugar, wine, dark soy and chicken broth and stir fry for 5 minutes.

Add the drained beancurd, lower the heat and cook gently for 5 minutes. Sprinkle the ground Sichuan peppercorns over the top and stir them through the pork sauce. Serve with steamed jasmine rice.

P.S. Reinvent this dish as a first course or light supper by steaming whole beancurd squares over simmering water for 10 minutes. Make the pork sauce in the wok, arrange a square of beancurd on each warmed serving platter, and spoon the chilli pork sauce on top. Top with coriander and serve.

Feeds four.

Goat's cheese bruschetta

A heart-warming supper, teamed with a sharply dressed salad and a fresh pinot noir. Try to find a fresh goat's cheese such as that of Gabrielle Kervella of Fromage Fermier, which grills beautifully on the outside while becoming light and almost fluffy inside.

1 garlic clove
a few sprigs of fresh thyme
2 tbsp extra virgin olive oil
4 fresh goat's cheese rounds
4 thick slices of sourdough bread

Smash garlic and half the thyme leaves together, and leave in olive oil to infuse for an hour.

Grill goat's cheese rounds under a hot grill, without turning or moving, until lightly golden.

Brush bread with the flavoured olive oil and grill on both sides. Use an egg slice to gently remove goat's cheese rounds and place them on grilled bread.

Serve with a few extra sprigs of fresh thyme.

Feeds four.

Fish steak sandwich

Big, firm-fleshed deep-sea fish like tuna, swordfish and cod should be treated with as much respect as aged rump and fillet steak. Grill quickly and tuck into warm bread with rocket leaves and aioli (garlic mayonnaise).

1 eggplant (aubergine)
2 red peppers (capsicums)
2 zucchini
4 tbsp olive oil
4 small steaks of swordfish or blue eye
1 loaf Turkish pide bread or focaccia
1 bunch rocket, washed and dried
4 tbsp aioli (Broths and Sauces, 206)
1 lemon, quartered

Slice eggplant lengthwise, sprinkle with salt and leave for 1 hour to draw out any bitter juices. Rinse well and pat dry.

Cut red peppers lengthwise into quarters, discarding seeds and core. Cut zucchini lengthwise into thin strips.

Brush vegetables with olive oil and grill on both sides, turning once, until cooked.

Brush fish steaks with olive oil. Grill or pan-fry on both sides, turning once, leaving them nice and juicy inside.

Grill bread until warmed through. Top the base slices with rocket leaves, then layer red pepper, eggplant, zucchini, fish, then eggplant, red pepper and zucchini. Top with a spoonful of aioli and remaining bread.

Serve with lemon quarters.

Feeds four.

Salmon fish cakes

A luxurious version of the fish cakes of North-eastern England, bound with mashed potato and egg, crumbed and fried until golden. Fresh salmon makes this a very classy dish that deserves a decent bottle of wine and a well-dressed young green salad on the side.

400 g (14 oz) fresh salmon, filleted and skinned
sea salt and freshly ground black pepper
1 tbsp freshly chopped parsley
400 g (14 oz) mashed potatoes, without cream or butter
1 cup plain flour
3 eggs, beaten
1 cup fresh dry breadcrumbs
1 tbsp butter
1 tbsp olive oil
lemon butter sauce (Broths and Sauces, 209)
1 tbsp finely chopped chives

Heat oven to 180°C (350°F). Place salmon on a lightly oiled baking tray, sprinkle with salt and pepper and cover with foil. Cook for 8 to 10 minutes until fish is just firm outside, and still pink inside. Break up the salmon pieces with a fork, and mix with salt, pepper and parsley. Fold in most of the mashed potato, then continue adding it a spoonful at a time until you have a binding texture. Chill mixture until ready to use.

Shape fish cakes by packing the mixture into an egg ring. Dip into a bowl of flour, then a bowl of beaten egg, then a bowl of breadcrumbs, until completely coated.

Heat butter and oil in a frypan and cook fish cakes on one side until golden brown, before turning. Cook the other side lightly, making sure the fish cakes are cooked through.

Serve with lemon butter sauce spiked with finely chopped fresh chives.

P.S. For a lighter supper in warm weather, replace the lemon butter sauce with a vinaigrette of extra virgin olive oil, lemon juice, diced tomatoes and torn basil leaves.

Feeds four.

Marmitako

A colourful stew of tuna and peppers from the Basque region (I am told it is the country of my ancestors) between Spain and France. I depart from tradition – or at least common practice – to cook the tuna at the last moment so it remains tender and pink in the centre. It must be one of those contrary Basque separatist sort of things that's in the blood.

1 green pepper (capsicum)
1 red pepper (capsicum)
4 tomatoes
4 medium potatoes
750 g (1½ lb) tuna
2 tbsp olive oil
2 garlic cloves, crushed
1 onion, chopped
1 cup white wine
sea salt and freshly ground black pepper
1 tsp Spanish paprika

Cut peppers in half, remove seeds, and cut flesh into strips. Dunk tomatoes in a pot of simmering water for 15 seconds and peel off skin. Cut in half, squeeze out seeds, and chop remaining flesh.

Peel potatoes and chop into small cubes. Clean and dry the tuna, trim off any skin or dark red blood lines, and cut into bite-sized cubes.

Heat olive oil in frypan and cook garlic, onion and peppers, stirring, for 10 minutes. Add tomatoes, potatoes, wine, salt, pepper and paprika. Cover and simmer gently for 45 minutes until potatoes are soft, stirring occasionally, and adding half a cup of water if it appears dry. Crush a few of the cooked potatoes into the sauce and stir well, to thicken it.

Add tuna and cook for 1 minute until tuna just changes colour on outside. Serve in warmed shallow soup or pasta bowls.

Feeds four.

Salt cod with creamed leeks

Buy your salt cod in an Italian (ask for *baccala*), Greek (*bakaliaros*) or Spanish (*bacalao*) deli, and don't be dismayed by the time it takes to soak out the salt. Within a day you will be tucking into a creamy, luscious fish dish thickened with potato and sweetened with leeks. Top with a poached egg for a perfect supper.

500 g (1 lb) salt cod
3 leeks
3 potatoes
2 tbsp butter
2 tbsp whipping (thickened) cream
freshly ground black pepper
2 tbsp finely chopped parsley
4 eggs

Soak salt cod for 24 hours in cold water, changing the water 3 times. Drain and place salt cod in a large pan. Cover with cold water, and bring to the boil. Lower heat and poach gently for 15 to 20 minutes. Drain fish, reserving the cooking liquid. Peel off skin and use your fingers to shred the fish into small flakes, removing all bones.

Trim leeks, wash well and cut into 5 cm (2 in) lengths. Cut each length in half lengthwise, and cut each half lengthwise into 4. Cut across to form tiny dice. Peel potatoes and slice into 1 cm (½ in) slices, then cut into small cubes.

Melt butter in a frypan and cook leeks gently for 10 minutes until soft. Add potatoes and 500 ml (18 fl oz) of the reserved cooking liquid. Cook gently for 20 minutes or until potatoes are soft and tender. Mash the potatoes in the pan with a potato masher until squashed.

Add the flaked fish, cream, black pepper and parsley and heat through gently.

Poach eggs according to recipe in Pantry (page 216). Serve salt cod and leeks in four shallow soup or pasta bowls, and top each dish with a poached egg. Serve with hot toast on the side.

Feeds four.

Risi e bisi

It's not a risotto, nor is it a soup, but some Venetian concept in between that is slightly soupy but should still be able to be eaten with a fork. Risi e bisi (rice and peas) used to be served on April 25th at the annual feast of San Marco, the patron saint of Venice, in celebration of the first springtime peas from the kitchen gardens of the Venetian lagoons.

4 slices prosciutto or pancetta
2 tbsp butter
1 tbsp extra virgin olive oil
1 onion, finely chopped
2 tbsp finely chopped parsley
2 cups fresh, shelled peas
1 tsp sugar
6 cups hot chicken broth
300 g (11 oz) arborio rice
salt and freshly ground black pepper
3 tbsp freshly grated Parmigiano cheese

Chop prosciutto or pancetta into small squares.

Melt butter and olive oil in a heavy-bottomed pan. Add prosciutto or pancetta, onion and parsley, and cook for 5 to 10 minutes, until onion is soft. Add peas, sugar and 2 cups of hot chicken broth, and cook gently for 10 to 15 minutes. Add remaining hot chicken broth and bring to the boil. Add rice, salt and pepper and cook gently, stirring occasionally, until the rice is tender but not mushy (around 20 to 30 minutes).

Remove from the heat, stir in grated cheese and serve in wide, shallow soup bowls.

Feeds four.

Soba noodles with salmon

A light, clean, healthy bowl of soba noodles topped with grilled teriyaki salmon is the perfect supper dish, quick to do and easy to digest.

400 g (14 oz) soba noodles
1 knob of fresh ginger
4 small salmon fillets, skinned
1 bunch of spinach, washed and stemmed
4 green (spring) onions, sliced on the diagonal

Dashi broth
1.5 litre (3 pints) water
15 g (½ oz) instant dashi powder
2 tbsp soy sauce
2 tbsp mirin

Teriyaki sauce
2 tbsp dark soy sauce
1 tbsp sake
1 tbsp mirin
1 tsp sugar
1 tbsp peanut oil

Combine soy, sake, mirin, sugar and oil in a small pot and heat, stirring, until sugar has dissolved. Set aside.

Heat water in a second pot, and add dashi powder, soy and mirin. Peel ginger, cut into cubes and crush in a garlic press until you have 1 tablespoon of ginger juice. Add juice to the broth, and adjust flavourings to taste.

Cook noodles in plenty of boiling, salted water until al dente (about 8 minutes). Drain and rinse in cold water. Cover with plastic and set aside.

Brush salmon with teriyaki sauce and grill quickly, on an oiled grill, leaving the inside lightly pink. Bring broth to just below the boil. Add noodles for 30 seconds to heat through, then divide noodles between 4 warmed bowls. Dip spinach leaves briefly into the broth to wilt them, and divide among bowls.

Ladle hot broth into each bowl, and top noodles with grilled salmon. Scatter green onions on top and serve with chopsticks and spoons.

Feeds four.

Mozza in carrozza

'Mozza' is my nickname for that gentle, fresh Italian mozzarella cheese, traditionally made from buffalo milk, and a *carrozza* is a carriage, used to signify the carriage-wheel shape of these very suppery pan-fried sandwiches.

8 thin slices of good bread, crusts removed
8 slices fresh bocconcini mozzarella, 1 cm (½ in) thick
4 anchovy fillets, drained and rinsed
pinch of dried or fresh oregano
3 eggs, beaten
sea salt and freshly ground black pepper
vegetable or olive oil for frying

Lay out 4 slices of bread. Top each with a single layer of sliced mozzarella. Cut each anchovy in half lengthwise, and top each slice with half an anchovy and a little oregano. Top with remaining bread.

Stamp out 4 round sandwiches with a cookie cutter, egg-ring or rim of a glass. Pinch the edges together lightly and flatten lightly with your hand. Beat eggs in a bowl with salt and pepper until well mixed. Soak the sandwiches in beaten egg on both sides.

Heat a thin layer of oil in a frypan, until it just starts to smoke. Add sandwiches and fry on both sides until the outside is lightly golden and the cheese has started to melt. Drain on paper towel, and serve hot.

Feeds four.

Meat loaf

The sort of people who love this the most are those who grew up with not enough, and now have too much. It's as if they are punishing themselves for their success. Serve this lighter version of the humble meat loaf with mashed potato and home-made tomato sauce for the complete experience.

1 kg (2 lb) veal and pork mince
250 g (9 oz) chicken mince
½ red pepper (capsicum), finely diced
1 onion, finely diced
5 slices bread, soaked in milk and squeezed dry
3 eggs, beaten
1 tbsp chopped parsley
1 tbsp dried breadcrumbs
pinch of cayenne pepper
½ tsp ground nutmeg
60 ml (2 fl oz) tomato sauce or ketchup
2 tsp Worcestershire sauce

Heat oven to 190°C (375°F). Chuck everything into a huge bowl. Mix well with your hands until well mixed and a little gluey. Oil a large oblong 1 litre (1¾ pint) loaf tin or terrine, fill with mixture and cover with foil. Place on a tray and bake for 1 hour, to get the juices going.

Remove foil and tip out two-thirds of the juices that have gathered. Return to the oven and bake, uncovered, for a further hour, until the top is crusty brown and the meat is cooked through.

Remove from oven and leave to rest for 5 or 10 minutes. Remove from the tin and cut into hearty slices.

Serve with home-made tomato sauce (Broths and Sauces, 210) and a good salad.

Feeds eight.

Pipérade

Bright red and yellow peppers and creamy scrambled eggs – we must be in the Basque provinces, eating pipérade at suppertime. I like to keep the pipérade separate from the eggs rather than combining them in a more traditional omelette, when the eggs go an alarming shade of pink. Serve with thin slices of jamon, prosciutto or thin Bayonne-style ham on the side.

2 red peppers (capsicum)
2 yellow peppers (capsicum)
2 ripe tomatoes
2 tbsp good olive oil
2 onions, thinly sliced into rings
8 eggs
2 tbsp thickened cream
sea salt and freshly ground black pepper
1 tbsp butter
dash of olive oil

Cut peppers in half, and discard membrane and seeds. Slice into long, very thin strips.

Dunk tomatoes in a pot of simmering water for 10 seconds, then remove and peel off skin. Cut in half and squeeze out and discard seeds. Chop tomato flesh roughly.

Heat olive oil in a heavy-bottomed frypan. Add peppers and onions and cook for 20 minutes until softened. Add tomatoes and cook for another 5 minutes, then cover and cook until any juices have evaporated.

Beat eggs, cream, salt and pepper together in a bowl.

Heat butter and olive oil in a frypan and add eggs. Cook over low heat, stirring slowly and constantly, until soft and creamy. Divide eggs between warmed serving plates (on toast if you like), and surround with pipérade.

Feeds four.

Tapas

This is not a wonderful, civilised way to eat. It is a wonderful, civilised way to drink.
The food was originally placed on top of one's glass to keep out the flies, and it simply became second nature –
and common sense – to eat as one drank.
But it is far more important to drink, gossip, do business, flirt, cut a charming figure and move on to the next tapas bar
around the corner, than it is to just eat and drink.
To make tapas at home is to taste only the physical manifestation, not the emotional, unless you invite around three hundred
strangers, pack them into your smallest room, hang the rafters with legs of ham, and keep the party going all night long.
Mind you, the flavours of tapas are pungent and seductive and translate well to eating at home, even on your own.
Golden saffron, punchy garlic, crisp almonds, fruity olive oil, peppery pimentos, spicy sausages, fresh apple cider and
fragrant jamon (ham) have an age-old synergy that makes them natural complements to each other, and to a glass of
plummy Rioja wine or a nutty, bone-dry Amontillada sherry.
The best tapas are drop-dead simple:
marinated sardines, and lightly pickled baby octopus (Salad, 77);
paprika-laden chorizo sausages;
tiny meatballs in tomato sauce;
an earthenware pot of garlicky prawns;
salted cod and olives on crusty bread;
a wedge of warm, juicy potato tortilla;
or just a few slices of Serrano-style ham and a few tiny green arbequina olives.
But anything will work, as long as it is taken standing up,
in a crowded room,
leaning against a good friend.

Sardines in vinegar

Rinse 500 g (1 lb) fresh sardine fillets in cold water and pat dry with paper towel.
Arrange in a shallow glass or earthenware dish.
Add 1 cup white vinegar and 3 tbsp water, cover with plastic wrap and refrigerate overnight.
Drain off the vinegar, and arrange sardines neatly on serving plate.
Scatter with 1 dsp sea salt, 2 finely sliced garlic cloves and 2 tbsp finely chopped parsley,
and drizzle with 4 to 5 tbsp fruity olive oil.
Serve with crusty bread and roasted red peppers, to pile onto lightly grilled slices of crusty breadstick.
Top with caper berries or a few capers.
Serve with cold beer or a freshly opened, well chilled bottle of Jerez (sherry).
Feeds four to six as part of a tapas meal.

Not everything needs a sauce.

To hear a French chef speak of a sauce as the jewel in the crown, the final symphony, or the pearl necklace on the throat of a beautiful woman, as if no food is complete without a sauce – and no beautiful woman is complete without pearls – is to giggle hysterically while tucking into one's immaculately unsauced steak, fish or chicken.

But sometimes, you've grilled the steak, fried the schnitzel, or seared the salmon, and it's still not turning you on.

You need that little something extra that makes the difference between the everyday and the wow-what-was-that?

When you find the time and the place for a good sauce, don't deny it.

With it, you can add contrasting and complementing flavours, colours and scents,

disguise a delicious but boringly brown sludge of something,

spike up a bland flavour with a piquant one,

link two or three disparate ingredients on a plate,

or just make a witty bow to tradition with a classic sauce on an otherwise modern meal.

It gives the burger its relish, the pie its tomato sauce, the roast lamb its gravy, and the apple pie its pool of custard.

Sauces of the past used to be thickened with a beurre manié of flour, or rich liaisons, bound with egg yolks, butter, cream and breadcrumbs, but flavour has taken over from texture, and a simple vinaigrette of oil and vinegar flavoured with herbs, a puréed vegetable hit with a pinch of spice, or crushed lemon grass and chilli in Asian fish sauce is now enough of a statement.

If a sauce frames the dish with a flavour, then a broth is the canvas upon which you – oops,

nearly fell into a pot of hyperbole myself.

Far better to say that a good broth is the best start to a meal that a cook can have.

With it, you need no other flavour booster, no additives, and no strange little cubed things.

But not everything needs to be based on a veal, chicken, fish or vegetable broth.

Some things just don't need the extra help.

There are vegetables that need only water to transform them into soup,

and vegetable and bean purées and that need only a little butter or oil to emulsify them into luscious, glossy things of beauty.

So if you still think your meal is nothing without the kick of flavour from a broth or that final, glamorous, saucy accessory:

go buy yourself some pearls.

Broths and Sauces

Aioli
Bread sauce
Dashi broth
Soy dipping sauce
Vegetable broth
Apple sauce
Fish broth
Toffee sauce
Chicken broth
Cumberland sauce
Ponzu sauce
Mum's gravy
Teriyaki sauce
Sesame sauce
Hot chocolate sauce
Peanut sauce
Mayonnaise
Lemon butter sauce
Cheese sauce
Tomato sauce
Nuoc cham sauce
Tomato and basil sauce
Pouring custard

Aioli

The Provençal French aioli – and the original Catalan alioli – needs warm sunshine, garlic and olive oil. Eaten outdoors with the sun on your back and cool wine in your glass, aioli becomes much more than just a garlicky mayonnaise. Serve with a bowl of small, steamed potatoes for lunch, or on top of char-grilled vegetables or salmon for dinner.

8 garlic cloves, peeled
2 egg yolks
½ tsp sea salt
300 ml (10 fl oz) good, fruity olive oil
2 tbsp lemon juice

Crush garlic and sea salt in a mortar until mushy. Beat in the egg yolks until you have a creamy paste. Add the olive oil, drop by drop from a teaspoon, beating constantly, until you have a thickened paste. Beat in the lemon juice. Continue to add olive oil, as you continue to beat, until all the oil is absorbed and emulsified. Add extra lemon juice, salt and pepper to taste. (If aioli is too thick, beat in a tablespoon of warm water.)
P.S. If the aioli separates, place an extra egg yolk in a clean, dry bowl and beat in a spoonful of the aioli. Continue beating and adding aioli until it has regained its equilibrium.
Feeds four.

Bread sauce

An old English favourite with roasted game. At its simplest it can be used to nap a couple of roasted quail or small spatchcock. It is also quite divine with a simple roast chicken.

2 cloves
1 onion
400 ml (14 fl oz) milk
1 bay leaf
sea salt and freshly ground black pepper
4 thick slices of white bread
2 tbsp butter
1 tbsp cream

Stick cloves into the onion and place in a saucepan with milk, bay leaf, sea salt and pepper. Bring milk to just below boiling point, then reduce heat and simmer gently for 5 minutes. Cover, and remove from heat. Leave for an hour to infuse. Cut off crusts and whizz bread to soft white crumbs in a blender. Measure out 1 cup of crumbs and set aside. Remove onion, cloves and bay leaf from milk and discard. Heat milk gently, gradually stirring in the crumbs, the butter and the cream. Cook for about 15 minutes, stirring occasionally, until sauce is smooth and thick.
Makes 350 ml (12 fl oz).

Dashi broth

First, make your dashi (or buy instant dashi at a Japanese supermarket). Then, a beautiful, simple, aesthetically pleasing Japanese meal is only minutes away.

1 litre (1¾ pints) water
25 g (1 oz) konbu seaweed
25 g (1 oz) bonito flakes

Add konbu to cold water in saucepan and slowly heat the water. Remove konbu just before the water reaches boiling point. Add bonito flakes, remove from the heat as soon as the water boils, and strain.
Makes 1 litre (1¾ pints).

Soy dipping sauce

Dark soy is an aged soy that is actually lighter in salt than light soy sauce. The use of 'cooked' oil has long been a kitchen secret of Cantonese sauces.

2 tbsp peanut or vegetable oil
3 tbsp dark soy sauce
3 tbsp light soy sauce
1 slice ginger, cut into matchsticks
1 red chilli, finely sliced

Heat oil until it starts to smoke. Remove from heat and allow to cool. Mix cooked oil with dark and light soy, ginger and chilli. Serve in small dipping bowls.
Makes half a cup.

Vegetable broth

A light, fresh base for sauces or soups that is an absolute dream to have ready and waiting in your refrigerator or freezer.

2 tomatoes
1 tbsp butter
2 brown onions, finely chopped
2 carrots, finely chopped
2 celery stalks with leaves, finely chopped
6 parsley stalks
6 cups boiling water

Cut tomatoes in half, squeeze out the seeds, and finely chop. Melt butter in a heavy-bottomed pot, add vegetables, parsley stalks and tomatoes, and cook for 5 minutes. Add 6 cups of boiling water, bring back to the boil, and simmer for 10 minutes. Strain broth through a sieve, cool and refrigerate.
Makes 1.5 litres (3 pints).

Apple sauce

With the right apples, you will need neither water nor sugar to create a light, fluffy, buttery apple sauce. Serve with roast pork, cold ham, or plain old grilled sausages.

4 granny smith apples
2 tbsp butter
½ tsp ground nutmeg

Peel and core apples, and cut into slices. Melt butter in a heavy-bottomed pan. Add apple and cook gently, covered, shaking the pan occasionally. Remove from heat when the apple collapses, as it virtually implodes into a sauce. Add nutmeg and stir lightly. Serve warm or cold.
Makes one cup.

Fish broth

If you get into the habit of buying whole fish, you will always have a few heads and bones to whip up a quick fish broth for the table or the freezer.

1 onion
1 carrot
1 celery stalk
1 garlic clove
1 leek, white part only
1 tbsp olive oil
1 kg (2 lb) fish heads and bones
1 cup dry white wine
10 peppercorns
2 bay leaves
1 litre (1¾ pints) water

Chop onion, carrot, celery, garlic and leek. Heat oil in large pot and cook vegetables over low heat for about 10 minutes until they 'sweat'. Add rinsed fish heads and bones, wine, peppercorns and bay leaves and bring to boil. Add water and return to the boil. Simmer over low heat for 15 minutes, no longer. Strain through a strainer lined with muslin, pushing down on the bones to release the utmost juices.
Makes 1 litre (1¾ pints).

Toffee sauce

The famous sticky toffee sauce, ready to pour over steamed puddings, cakes, and poached fruits.

150 g (5¼ oz) soft brown sugar
1 cup thickened cream
½ tsp vanilla extract
1 tbsp butter

Combine the sugar, cream, vanilla extract and butter in a saucepan. Bring to the boil, stirring. Reduce heat and simmer for 5 minutes. Set aside and reheat when needed.
Feeds four.

Chicken broth

The trick to a great broth is not to be scared of chicken feet and giblets. They make it great. The second trick is that your own feet need to stay planted by the stove as you skim, for a gorgeously clear result. If you want a more intense flavour, cook again at a high simmer to reduce liquid by half.

2 kg (4 lb) chicken bones
1 kg (2 lb) chicken feet and giblets (optional)
3 litres (5¼ pints) water
2 onions, halved
2 carrots, roughly chopped
1 celery stalk, roughly chopped
3 parsley stalks
8 peppercorns
1 bay leaf
1 leek, white part only

Rinse chicken bones, feet and giblets and place them in your largest pot with water. Bring to the boil, and skim off any froth that rises to the surface. Add remaining ingredients, and simmer for 3 hours, uncovered, skimming occasionally. Strain into a bowl, discarding bones and vegetables. Chill overnight to allow any fat to rise to the surface. Remove fat and broth is ready to use or to freeze.
Makes 2 litres (3½ pints).

Cumberland sauce

A very traditional English jelly that goes well with poached tongue and cold meats.

orange rind
3 tbsp redcurrant jelly
1 tsp mustard powder
150 ml (5¼ fl oz) port
1 tbsp orange juice
1 tbsp lemon juice

Scrape the white pith from a 10 cm (4 in) length of orange rind, and cut into thin matchsticks. Combine rind and 1 cup of water in a small pot and bring to the boil. Simmer gently for 15 minutes. Add redcurrant jelly and heat through gently, stirring. Add mustard powder, port, orange juice and lemon juice. Cook gently for 5 minutes, stirring well. Strain into a small bowl and allow to cool.
Makes around 200 ml (7 fl oz).

Ponzu sauce

A classic Japanese sauce that is exquisite with oysters, delicate shellfish and fish. It will last a long time, and gain complexity over the months.

2 tbsp mirin
300 ml (10 fl oz) light soy sauce
4 tbsp white rice vinegar
125 ml (4 fl oz) lemon juice
1 tbsp flaked bonito
1 piece konbu seaweed

Heat mirin in a small pan over gentle heat until bubbling. Combine mirin with soy, vinegar, lemon juice, bonito flakes and konbu and set aside in a cool place for 24 hours. Strain sauce and store in a sterilised jar or bottle.
Makes 500 ml (18 fl oz).

Mum's gravy

Mum always used the scraped-up pan drippings, a sprinkling of flour, a spoonful of Vegemite (yeast extract) for colour and salt content and any available broth (or the water from cooking the vegetables) for the best gravy in the world. 'You have to stay there and look after it until the flour is really browned,' she says. 'You can't walk away from it.'

2 tbsp roasting juices, in roasting pan
 or 2 tbsp butter, or rendered chicken fat or bacon fat
2 tbsp plain flour
600 ml (1 pint) hot broth
1 tsp Vegemite
fresh thyme leaves

Heat pan on top of the stove, scraping any meaty, burnt bits of meat from the base of the pan with a wooden spoon or spatula. Sprinkle with flour, and stir and scrape over gentle heat to colour it a light golden brown, but be careful of burning. When it is really messy and grungy-looking, after about 5 minutes, add the hot broth, stirring quickly. Add Vegemite, if using, and thyme leaves and stir well. Adjust consistency according to how thin or thick you like your gravy. Continue to simmer and reduce in volume if too thin. Add more water or broth if too thick. Strain and serve in a warmed sauce boat.
Makes 500 ml (18 fl oz).

Teriyaki sauce

Go beyond Japanese cooking with your teriyaki sauce, and brush it over grilled salmon and steaks at the last moment.

6 tbsp sake
6 tbsp mirin
6 tbsp dark soy sauce
1 tbsp sugar

Combine sake, mirin, dark soy and sugar in a small pot. Heat over moderate heat, stirring, until sugar dissolves. Use now, or cool and keep refrigerated until use.
Makes one cup.

Sesame sauce

Medical evidence refutes it, but I insist that this classic Japanese accompaniment of ground sesame seeds is addictive, especially served with lightly cooked spinach.

3 tbsp white sesame seeds
1 tsp sugar
1 tbsp dark soy sauce
3 tbsp dashi broth (page 206)

Heat sesame seeds in a dry non-stick fry pan or wok until they smell toasty, being careful not to burn. Set aside one good pinch of seeds, and grind the rest to a paste in a mortar with pestle. Add sugar and mix well. Add soy sauce and dashi and mix well. Serve in small bowls. Sprinkle with remaining pinch of sesame seeds.
Feeds four as a dipping sauce.

Hot chocolate sauce

Just what you want when you want a hot chocolate sauce to pour over vanilla bean ice cream, or poached pears, or just about anything, really.

150 g (5¼ oz) dark bitter chocolate or couverture
150 ml (5¼ fl oz) thickened (whipping) cream
½ tsp vanilla extract
2 tbsp butter

Break chocolate up into small pieces. Combine chocolate, cream, vanilla and butter in a heat-proof bowl set over a pot of simmering water. Stir constantly as the chocolate gradually melts. Serve hot.
Makes around one cup.

Peanut sauce

Satay is not the reason we love satay. The sauce is. This is the must-have accompaniment to satay, curry puffs and gado gado.

1 tbsp tamarind pulp
2 tbsp boiling water
200 g (7 oz) roasted peanuts
4 dried chillies, soaked in water
4 shallots, peeled
2 garlic cloves
4 candlenuts or macadamia nuts
1 stalk lemon grass, peeled and sliced
2 tbsp oil
250 ml (9 fl oz) coconut milk
2 tbsp palm or brown sugar
1 tsp salt

Soak tamarind in hot water for 10 minutes, then squeeze and knead until dissolved. Strain and set tamarind water aside. Pound or whizz peanuts until fine. Pound, grind or whizz drained chillies, shallots, garlic cloves, nuts, and lemon grass into a paste. Heat oil and fry paste for 3 minutes. Add coconut milk and bring to the boil, stirring constantly. Add tamarind water, sugar, ground peanuts and salt to taste and cook for 5 minutes. If too thick, thin with a little water.
Makes around one cup.

Mayonnaise

You can make mayonnaise in the blender, as here, or in a bowl with a wire whisk. Either way, just remember to add the olive oil as slowly as humanly possible as you blend/whisk. Once the oil has been emulsified into a creamy dressing, you can add a little Dijon mustard, some cumin, roasted garlic, fresh herbs, chilli sauce, or whatever you like for more fun and flavour. Use on seafoods and salads.

2 egg yolks
1 tbsp lemon juice
375 ml (13 fl oz) light olive oil
sea salt and freshly ground black pepper

Blend egg yolks and lemon juice in food processor. Keep motor running while you slowly, drop by drop, pour in a tablespoon of olive oil. Continue adding oil very slowly, until half the olive oil has been absorbed. Now, drizzle the oil in slightly faster, teaspoon by teaspoon, until all oil is absorbed. Taste for salt and pepper, and add more lemon juice if you like it sharper or thinner.
Makes one and a half cups.

Lemon butter sauce

A tangy golden sauce that lifts any fish dish, particularly salmon, and is adorable over asparagus. The butter should be very cold, almost frozen, or the sauce will not emulsify.

2 tbsp lemon juice
60 ml (2 fl oz) chicken or vegetable broth
150 g (5¼ oz) cold butter, cut into tiny dice
sea salt and freshly ground black pepper

Combine lemon juice and chicken or vegetable stock in a small saucepan, stirring. Bring to a simmer, and whisk in the well-chilled butter a few small pieces at a time, without allowing the sauce to boil. Taste for lemon juice, add salt and pepper and serve at once.
Makes three-quarters of a cup.

Cheese sauce

There is not too much call for a béchamel sauce these days, unless it is in an Italian lasagne or Greek moussaka (in which case use the Greek kefalotyri cheese to flavour it). Don't be scared to make it a light sauce, by adding as much liquid as the 'roux', formed from amalgamating the butter and flour, will take. Or replace the cheese with two tablespoons of finely chopped parsley, and pour over corned beef, vegetables or fish dishes.

2 tbsp butter
3 tbsp flour
2 cups milk
pinch of grated nutmeg
pinch of ground cinnamon
2 tbsp grated parmesan or kefalotyri cheese
sea salt and freshly ground black pepper

Melt butter in a saucepan. Remove from heat and add flour. Return to a very low heat, stirring constantly with a wooden spoon for 3 or 4 minutes until it just starts to colour; the idea being to 'cook' the flour so it doesn't taste raw, without browning it. Add milk all at once, and bring to the boil, stirring constantly. Allow to bubble gently for 5 minutes, until it starts to thicken. You want it thick enough to coat the spoon, rather than drippy or solid. Stir in nutmeg, cinnamon, cheese, salt and pepper, and keep warm until serving.
Makes 500 ml (18 fl oz).

Tomato sauce

'Congratulations,' he said, when I first made this sauce. 'You've succeeded in making something that tastes a lot like Heinz Tomato Sauce'. 'Goody', I replied. 'That makes it perfect for my cabbage rolls and meat loaf.'

2 tbsp olive oil
1 onion, chopped
1 celery stalk, chopped
1 carrot, chopped
1 tbsp flour
500 ml (18 fl oz) chicken broth
350 ml (12 fl oz) can of tomato pulp or tomatoes with juices
2 tbsp tomato paste
2 tsp soft brown sugar

Heat oil and fry onion, celery and carrot for 10 minutes. Sprinkle with flour, and cook over gentle heat, stirring and scraping with a wooden spoon, until flour is lightly browned. Add a little of the chicken broth, stirring well, then slowly add remaining chicken broth, stirring constantly. Add tomato pulp or tomatoes, tomato paste and sugar and bring to the boil, stirring. Reduce heat and simmer for 30 minutes. Serve over cabbage rolls or sliced meat loaf. For a finer sauce, push through a sieve or mouli before serving.
Feeds four.

Nuoc cham sauce

The ubiquitous sauce of Vietnam; a little salty, a little sweet and a little hot in every mouthful. No wonder it is ubiquitous.

2 small red chillies, chopped
2 garlic cloves
1 tbsp palm sugar
2 tbsp lime or lemon juice
1 tbsp rice wine vinegar
4 tbsp Thai fish sauce (nam pla)
3 tbsp water

Combine chillies, garlic and sugar in a mortar or tough bowl and pound or grind until smooth. Add lime or lemon juice, vinegar, fish sauce, and water, and stir well. Store in an airtight jar and keep in refrigerator until needed.
Makes half a cup.

Tomato and basil sauce

Make this whenever you find or grow great, ripe, sweet-smelling tomatoes – and then work out what to do with it. Use it as a pasta sauce in its own right, or as the base of a sauce, or serve as a puddle with a simple grill.

1 kg (2 lb) ripe roma tomatoes
5 tbsp olive oil
1 garlic clove, bruised
handful of basil leaves, torn
sea salt and freshly ground black pepper

Drop tomatoes into boiling water for 10 seconds, remove and peel. Cut them in half, squeeze out seeds, and chop remaining flesh. Heat olive oil and garlic in a saucepan. Add tomatoes, basil, salt and pepper, and cook for 20 minutes until the sauce thickens. Discard garlic. Add some extra basil leaves at the end of cooking to heighten the flavour.
Feeds four.

Pouring custard

There are some things that happen to you in childhood that you never quite get over, and a good custard is one of them. My mother used to make custard constantly, in her toughest old saucepan, resting the whole pot, with a sizzle, in the kitchen sink to stop it from cooking further and turning into scrambled eggs. If this is your first attempt at custard, fill the sink with cold water now. You may need it.

6 eggs yolks
85 g (3 oz) caster sugar
500 ml (18 fl oz) milk
1 vanilla bean, split lengthwise

Whisk egg yolks and sugar together for a few minutes until pale and creamy. When you lift the mixture with the whisk, it should fall back into the bowl in a ribbon-like stream without breaking. Bring milk and vanilla bean to boil, then scrape seeds from bean into milk and discard bean. Pour milk in a slow, steady stream into the egg mixture, whisking slowly. When mixture is combined, return it to the pan and cook very gently, stirring all the while with a wooden spoon for 10 to 15 minutes, until custard thickens enough to drip slowly from the spoon. If the mixture starts to set, remove from heat, strain, cool, and return to a gentler heat. Strain into a bowl resting in a sink or basin of ice-cold water. Cool and chill.
Makes two cups.

Remember the walk-in pantry? Of course you don't.

It was lined with jars of preserves and dusky spices, sacks of flour, grains, sugar and nuts, salt and pepper, strings and papers, combs of honey and baskets of onions, nuts and pumpkins; and bottles of olive oils and vinegars.

Necklaces of dried chillies, fresh garlic and herbs hung from the ceiling.

There was a shelf of baking needs, pastes, pickles and chutneys; fresh eggs – complete with feathers – resting on a cool marble slab, windfall baskets of fruit, rounds of cheese and squares of butter, tea leaves and coffee beans and all those things one had to 'store in a cool place' before we were duped into thinking the refrigerator was sent from heaven.

It was a room of stolen treats for children, and social security for adults.

It faced the right direction and kept a constant temperature, cool enough to keep winter apples in storage long into spring.

Today, our pantry is the walk-in gourmet deli, a place that kindly stores all the things we didn't know we needed until we walked in.

Good food stores do things for us.

They don't run out of pasta or canned tomatoes or olive oil the way we do.

They always have that special cheese, or those particular biscuits that we need.

But best of all, they are full of ideas that make our lives work.

Pick up Greek dips, Turkish bread, and masses of sliced prosciutto, and you can invite every one you know around for a drink.

Get some sourdough breads, smoked salmon, and a little caviar, and throw an instant cocktail party.

Grab a bottle of extra virgin olive oil, and tubs of glossy, marinated olives, midnight-black olive tapenade, lawn-green basil pesto, juicy semi-dried tomatoes and some pasta, risotto rice, or polenta, and you will be able to feed a frenzy of friends at any time.

Good food stores also have Asian noodles, soy sauce, hoi sin sauce, and rice wine; gourmet ice creams made of fresh fruit and eggs, and even home-made custards, crisp amaretti biscuits, and toffee sauces.

But our real pantry is our ability to do things for ourselves;

to make our own pasta, yoghurt and tomato jam;

to squeeze the cream from a coconut and the milk from almonds;

to emulsify eggs into mayonnaise with olive oil, and into a buttery curd with passionfruit pulp,

to dress a salad with a perfect vinaigrette,

to pickle our favourite vegetables,

to cook perfect rice

and to poach an immaculate egg every time we want one.

That way, we can walk into our own personal pantry any time we like, wherever we are, and we will always find something wonderful for dinner.

Just as it used to be.

Pantry

To caramelise lime and lemon rind
To cook rhubarb
To make almond milk
To cook rice
To poach an egg
To cook shellfish
To clarify butter
To dress a salad
To make yoghurt
To make chermoula
To make garlic breadcrumbs
To make hot chilli oil
To make laksa paste
To prepare tripe
To make tomato jam
To make roti jala
To make pastry cream
To make puff pastry
To make herbed yoghurt cheese
To make fragrant sugar
To make passionfruit curd
To obtain coconut cream
To pickle vegetables
To roast a chicken
To roast red peppers
To pickle beetroot
To frost grapes
To cut green onion flowers

To caramelise lime and lemon rind

A cute, playful garnish for cakes, tarts and anything tangy and citrusy. Use the syrup as a dressing for poached fruits, pour it over walnut, orange or poppy seed cake as a sweet, syrupy finish, or reduce it to a gorgeous caramel.

2 lemons
2 limes
juice of 1 lemon
1 cup caster sugar
1 cup water

Peel lemons and limes, and scrape off any white pith. Using the point of a very sharp knife, cut peel into long, extremely thin strips. Combine sugar and water in a heavy-bottomed pot, and bring to the boil, stirring until sugar dissolves. Add the strips of lemon and lime rind, and adjust the heat to a gentle simmer. Cook for 30 minutes until the rind becomes quite translucent and the syrup becomes sticky. Remove rind and drain on paper towel.
Makes enough rind to garnish one cake or four desserts.

To cook rhubarb

'Red celery' lends itself to just a slow braise in the oven, with no fierce boiling or added water necessary. Eat it for breakfast with fresh yoghurt, turn it into rhubarb pie, or serve it with roast duckling, pork or any rich meat. Trim of all the leaves, which are toxic, and use only the stalks.

500 g (1 lb) rhubarb
3 tbsp soft brown sugar

Heat oven to 180°C (350°F). Trim rhubarb stalks, discarding all leaves and ends. Wash stalks and dry. Cut in half lengthwise. Make a layer of rhubarb on the base of a baking dish and scatter with sugar. Bake for 30 minutes or until rhubarb is soft and a syrup has formed. Transfer to serving dish, trying to retain the natural shape, and drizzle with the syrupy juices.
Feeds four.

To make almond milk

Almonds must surely equal olives as 'a taste as old as time', and almond milk has surely given as great a pleasure as the juice of pressed olives.

250 g (9 oz) almonds, ground
500 ml (18 fl oz) water

Wrap ground almonds loosely in a piece of muslin. Pour water into a basin. Dip almond bag into water and leave for four hours. Squeeze muslin occasionally during this time to extract the 'milk'. Discard almonds and use almond milk for junkets, jellies, and custards.
Makes 500 ml (18 fl oz).

To cook rice

I love my rice cooker, because it is so set-and-forget and because it spreads the sweet smell of cooking rice all through the house, calling me into the kitchen for a pre-dinner drink. If you buy one, get yourself a heap of rice and cook it all weekend, to get your quantity of rice to water right (they're all a bit different). If you don't have one, turn an ordinary saucepan into a rice cooker. One cup of rice will cook into three cups of cooked rice, but always cook more rice than you think you will need, and people will always eat it.

2 cups raw white rice, e.g. jasmine

Place rice in a strainer and rinse under cold running water, until the water draining off is clear and not cloudy. Shake well and place in rice cooker or in a good strong saucepan with close-fitting lid. Add fresh cold water or a light, clear chicken or fish broth to cover rice from the fingertip of your index finger to the first knuckle (just stick your finger in until you feel the top of the rice, then keep adding water until it reaches the first knuckle). Turn on the rice cooker and it will do the rest. Or bring liquid to the boil in the saucepan, then cover the top with 2 sheets of baking paper or foil, and jam on the lid. Turn the heat to very low, using a heat dispersion pad if necessary, and cook for 20 minutes. Remove lid and check rice, which should be cooked and steaming. Fluff it up with 2 forks, being careful not to scrape at the bottom of the pan in case a little rice has stuck there and browned (probably). Transfer to a warm bowl and serve.
Feeds four.

To poach an egg

You will need a wide, shallow-sided stainless steel pan with a lid, a slotted spoon, some kitchen paper and a pair of scissors. After that, the perfect poached egg is only a matter of timing.

4 eggs (65 g), as fresh as possible
2 tbsp white wine vinegar

Fill pan with water to 5 cm (2 in) level and bring to a rolling boil (in which medium-sized bubbles appear on surface of water, but there is no turbulence below). Add vinegar, which will help the white coagulate. Crack open an egg and drop it quickly but carefully into the water. Repeat with remaining eggs. (If your egg white disappears into strands, the water is boiling too hard.) Bring the water back to the boil, then reduce immediately to a gentle simmer and cover pan with lid. Check after 3 minutes, and remove with a slotted spoon when whites have set. Drain on several folds of kitchen paper. Trim any messy edges with scissors and serve immediately.
Feeds two to four.

To cook shellfish

He cooks all the shellfish in our household, and turns it into a bit of a production, I might add. First, he seeks out live clams or mussels, kept in sea water, then he chooses clean-looking shells, so he doesn't have to scrub them, then he soaks them, changing the water diligently, and then he cooks them with such care and intimacy that he virtually names each one as it comes out of the cooking broth. His reward, apart from that of absolute freshness? I adore him.

1 kg (2 lb) clams or mussels
2 tbsp olive oil
2 garlic cloves, squashed flat
a few black peppercorns
a few parsley stems
100 ml (3½ fl oz) white wine

Soak shellfish in a large pot of cold water for a few hours, changing the water twice during that time, which will help reduce any saltiness. Drain, and scrub if necessary. Pull the little furry beards from the mussels just prior to cooking. Heat olive oil in a heavy-bottomed, lidded pan. Add garlic, pepper-corns, parsley stems and white wine and heat until bubbling. Add the drained shellfish, cover immediately, and leave over a high heat. After one minute, shake the pan as hard as you can, then remove lid and use tongs to remove any shellfish that have opened up. Cover the pan again and cook for another minute. Remove lid and pick out any more opened shellfish. Clams will virtually pop open as you look at them, making it quite a hectic time for a minute or two.
Continue the process until all shells have opened, and throw out any that don't, as they should not be used. Strain the broth through a layer of dampened muslin into a small bowl, and taste. Hopefully, it won't be too salty and will be able to be used in your recipe. If all this is too hard, then find someone who loves doing it, and marry them.
P.S. If you will be using the shellfish in an Asian dish, swap the olive oil for peanut or vegetable oil and the parsley stems for coriander stems, and consider throwing in some crushed lemon grass as well as the garlic.
Feeds four.

To clarify butter

By heating butter, the milk residues rise to the surface and can be discarded. It is these residues that are the first to burn when you cook with butter, so getting rid of them enables you to cook at a higher temperature without browning.

250 g (9 oz) butter

Melt butter slowly, in a small saucepan. Skim off the froth as it rises, until the butter is clear. Pour into an earthenware jar and cool. Cover and store in refrigerator until needed.
Makes 225 g (around 8 fl oz).

To dress a salad

This is the only vinaigrette recipe you need, for any salad you care to name. An entrepreneurial Frenchman in London, the Chevalier d'Albignac, popularised the idea of 'French dressing' throughout English society. You can change the vinegar (white or red wine vinegar, sherry, balsamic or lemon juice), the lemon rind (to orange rind, olives or garlic), and the mustard (to eschalots, anchovies or yoghurt), but it's still the only recipe you'll ever need.

2 tbsp champagne vinegar
½ tsp sea salt
¼ tsp freshly ground black pepper
½ tsp grated lemon rind
1 tsp Dijon mustard
5 tbsp extra virgin olive oil

Combine vinegar, salt, pepper, lemon rind and mustard in a bowl. Whisk in olive oil, slowly, until mixture thickens. Taste and adjust flavours accordingly. Use for seafood, greens and vegetable salads.
P.S. Often I add a dribble of whatever dry white wine I am drinking at the time of making the salad, or the oil from a jar of sun-dried tomatoes, whatever fresh herbs I like at the time, a few capers, or shavings of nutty Parmigiano. Note the 'or' is not an 'and'. With a good salad, less is more.
Makes enough for one large salad.

To make yoghurt

All you need is a wide-mouthed vacuum flask or a yoghurt-maker and a bit of good plain (unflavoured) acidophilus yoghurt to start you off, and you're set for life. As long as you eat lots of yoghurt, it's likely to be a very long one. Serve with ripe figs, a drizzle of honey and some crushed walnuts.

500 ml (18 fl oz) milk
3 tbsp natural acidophilus yoghurt

Bring milk to the boil, and let boil gently for 2 minutes, without frothing up too much. Remove from heat and cool to 'baby's milk' temperature. Milk should still be warm, but cool enough to hold your finger in it for a few seconds. Skim off any skin. Place yoghurt in a large bowl and beat or whisk until smooth and runny. Add a tablespoon of the warm milk and beat well. Add another tablespoon and beat well. Continue adding milk slowly, beating until well mixed. Pour mixture into flask, and seal. Leave without opening for 8 hours. (The longer you leave it, the more sour it will be). Remove from the flask when thick and curdy, and place in an airtight jar in refrigerator to chill before eating.
P.S. This will last for 4 days. When you are down to your last 3 tablespoons, make the next batch. If it doesn't set, your milk may have been too hot or too cold.
Makes 500 ml (18 fl oz).

To make chermoula

This is a wonderful marinade for fish, shellfish, lamb or chicken.

1 onion, grated
2 cloves garlic, smashed
1 tsp ginger, powdered
3 tbsp chopped fresh parsley
3 tbsp chopped fresh coriander
juice of 2 lemons
1 tsp ground cumin
1 tsp paprika
freshly ground black pepper
½ tsp salt
10 tbsp extra virgin olive oil

Combine onion, garlic, ginger, parsley, coriander, lemon juice, cumin, paprika, pepper and salt in a bowl. Add extra virgin olive oil, gradually, while beating with a wooden spoon. For a finer texture, whizz everything in food processor.
Makes two cups.

To make garlic breadcrumbs

Scatter a crown of these noble crumbs over any baked vegetable dish and put in the oven for a final crisping. Or just serve as a separate bowl with a simple meal of roast meats or game, and invite each guest to add breadcrumbs and sauce.

2 tbsp butter
1 garlic clove, crushed
1 cup fresh white breadcrumbs
1 tsp very finely chopped parsley
sea salt and freshly ground black pepper

Melt butter in pan until foaming. Reduce heat to low, and add the crumbs gradually, stirring with a wire whisk until crumbs have absorbed the butter and turned golden and crisp. Add parsley, salt and pepper, and serve.
Makes one cup.

To make hot chilli oil

A pure, hot oil for the chilli-driven, to add to or accompany Asian meals. Use very sparingly, and avoid contact with face and eyes when handling chillies.

125 ml (4 fl oz) fresh, clean vegetable oil
3 hot red dried chillies, chopped
½ tsp salt

Heat oil in wok and add chopped chillies and their seeds. Stir for two or three minutes until the oil turns the colour of the chillies. Add salt, stir well until dissolved and allow to cool. Strain out the chillies and their seeds, and store in a specially marked small bottle.
Makes 125 ml (4 fl oz).

To make laksa paste

The best laksa pastes are made in a big, heavy mortar, and are pounded with a pestle, a strong arm and about fifteen minutes to spare. Failing that, bung it all in the food processor.

1 onion, chopped
1 tbsp grated ginger
2 garlic cloves, crushed
2 stalks lemon grass, white part only
4 dried chillies, soaked in water
6 candlenuts or macadamia nuts
1 tbsp belacan (dried shrimp paste)
6 laksa or Asian mint leaves
1 tsp ground coriander
1 tsp paprika
1 tsp ground turmeric
1 tsp ground cumin
1 tsp sugar
1 tsp salt

Pound or blend the onion, ginger and garlic together. Roughly chop lemon grass. Drain chillies, squeeze dry and finely chop. Add lemon grass, chillies, nuts, belacan, laksa leaves, coriander, paprika, turmeric, cumin, sugar and salt and continue pounding for up to 15 minutes until you have a mushy paste. To turn the curry paste into a curry, fry it in a little oil until fragrant, gradually add some chicken stock and bring to the boil, then reduce heat and add some coconut milk. Gently poach whatever you want – chicken, fish, noodles, prawns – until cooked, and serve. See Vegetables, 136, for a recipe with wing beans.
Feeds four.

To prepare tripe

Most butchers will have prepared tripe, but it can be over-bleached and over-cooked. By doing your own, you have control over cooking times and additives.

1 kg (2 lb) raw honeycomb tripe
1 onion, roughly chopped
1 celery stalk, roughly chopped
1 carrot, roughly chopped
handful of parsley stalks

Wash tripe well under plenty of cold running water, and place in a large saucepan of cold, salted water. Bring to the boil, and blanch for 5 minutes. Drain and rinse tripe in cold running water, until cool enough to handle. Cut the tripe into thin strips as called for in the recipe, and place in a saucepan of water with roughly chopped onion, celery, carrot and parsley stalks. Bring to the boil, then reduce heat and simmer for 4 to 5 hours, or until it just starts to turn tender. Your tripe is now ready to use according to your recipe.
Feeds four.

To make tomato jam

The idea here is to reduce the tomatoes and garlic to a nice gooey sludgy paste. Serve with grilled lamb, chicken, cold meats and shepherd's pie.

3 kg (6 lb) roma tomatoes, diced
3 onions, cut in half and sliced
6 garlic cloves, crushed
300 ml (10 fl oz) vinegar
500 g (1 lb) brown sugar
1 tbsp salt
1 tbsp black peppercorns
1 tbsp whole allspice
1 tbsp freshly ground black pepper

Combine all ingredients in a large non-reactive pot. Stir occasionally as you bring to the boil. Reduce heat slightly and cook over medium heat at a slow boil, stirring occasionally to save it from sticking, 45 minutes to 1 hour, or until liquid is reduced. Allow to cool for 10 minutes, then pour into hot, sterilised jars (straight from the dishwasher is a neat idea) and cover. Leave for 3 weeks before opening, and store in refrigerator after opening.
Makes around two cups.

To make roti jala

These lacy Malaysian pancakes, made by dribbling batter in overlapping circles onto a hot skillet, were invented to dip into juicy curries or stuff with minced meats. You can achieve the exquisite effect in several ways – by piercing four very thin holes in an empty can, by using a squeezable tomato sauce dispenser, by partially blocking off the tip of a funnel with your finger, or by simply dipping your hand into the batter and letting it dribble off your fingers – an acquired skill.

1 cup plain flour
1/2 tsp salt
1 cup fresh milk or thin coconut milk
1 egg, well beaten
1 tsp oil
2 tbsp vegetable oil for frying

Sift flour and salt together. Add milk, egg and 1 tsp oil, and beat well until smooth. Allow to stand for 5 minutes. Heat a solid non-stick frying pan or skillet, and brush lightly with oil. Using one of the techniques above, dribble the batter in overlapping circles on the hot skillet to form a lacy effect. When pancake is set on top and curling at the edges, turn and cook for 30 seconds on other side, without browning. Remove and fold into quarters. Oil the pan lightly between each pancake, and stack folded pancakes between two folds of cloth to keep warm.
Makes six.

To make pastry cream

A rich and luscious filling for fresh fruit tarts or little pastries, known in France as crème pâtissière and in Italy as crema pasticcera.

500 ml (18 fl oz) milk
1 vanilla pod, split lengthways
6 egg yolks
175 g (6 oz) caster sugar
50 g (1¾ oz) plain flour or cornflour

Scrape the seeds from the vanilla bean into the milk in a small pan. Add bean and heat gently to boiling point. Whisk egg yolks, sugar and flour together in a small bowl until thick. Pour milk gently into the egg mixture, whisking lightly until smooth. Return the mixture to a clean pan and cook gently for a few minutes, stirring constantly, as the mixture heats and thickens. Boil gently for 1 minute, whisking constantly. Discard vanilla bean, and strain through a coarse sieve into a bowl. Cover with cling-wrap, pressing the plastic against the surface of the cream to prevent a skin from forming. Chill until required.
Makes enough to fill a 24 cm (9½ in) wide pastry tart base.

To make puff pastry

Puff pastry is magic, and like most magic, there are a few rules to remember to make it look like sleight of hand. (Use the thumbprint method described – it really works.)

225 g (8 oz) butter
225 g (8 oz) plain flour
pinch of salt
150 ml (5¼ fl oz) cold water
few drops of lemon juice

Melt 50 g (1¾ oz) of butter and allow to cool. Leave remaining butter out to soften. Sift flour and salt together in a large bowl, and make a hole in the centre. Add water, lemon juice and cooled, melted butter to the well, and stir with a wooden spoon until the mixture is amalgamated. Let rest for 20 minutes. Reserve an area of the kitchen for the next few hours so you don't have to keep cleaning up each time you work the pastry. Flour the bench well and roll out the pastry into the shape of a cross. Place remaining softened butter in the middle and fold over each pastry flap. Pat into a rectangle and chill for 10 minutes.
Roll out pastry until it is long and skinny, about 50 cm (20 in). Fold each end in, to meet in the centre, then fold once more into a double turn. Press your thumb marks into the left and right corners as it faces you, then cover in plastic and let rest for 15 minutes. Turn pastry so that your thumb imprints are both on the right hand side of the pastry, and roll out again, fold in again, mark with thumbs and chill. Repeat process twice more, then leave to rest for an hour or so before using. Roll out on a floured bench and trim to the shape you want.
Makes enough for a 24 cm (9½ in) pastry case.

To make herbed yoghurt cheese

A delicious brunchy dip for crisp biscuits or accompaniment to grilled pide bread and vegetable antipasto.

500 ml (18 fl oz) natural acidophilus yoghurt
1 tsp thyme sprigs
1 tsp finely chopped parsley

Mix yoghurt, herbs, salt and pepper. Dampen a doubled square of muslin or cheesecloth and squeeze dry. Place over a basin and pour yoghurt mixture on top. Draw up the edges, and tie with string. Hang yoghurt over the bowl to drip for four or five hours or overnight. Remove cloth, and chill yoghurt before serving.
Feeds four.

To make fragrant sugar

If you like to bake cakes and make desserts, keep a jar of spiced sugar on hand, and your recipe will start way ahead of the average. Use for simple things like making a sugar syrup.

1 kg (2 lb) caster sugar
1 vanilla pod
1 cinnamon stick

Pour sugar into a large airtight jar. Push both vanilla pod and cinnamon stick down into the sugar and store for 1 month before using.
Makes 1 kg (2 lb).

To make passionfruit curd

Present in every old-fashioned Australian backyard is the passionfruit vine, bursting into blossom and then purple-skinned fruit every summer. Their tangy pulp is the perfect match for crisp snowy meringues (see pavlova recipe in Sweets, 168).

175 g (6½ oz) sugar
100 g (3½ oz) butter
3 eggs, lightly beaten
pulp of 6 passionfruit

Combine sugar and butter in a heat-proof bowl set over a pot of simmering water. Stir well with a wooden spoon until smooth. Remove from heat and add lightly beaten eggs while stirring quickly. Add passionfruit pulp while stirring quickly. Return to a gentle heat, stirring constantly until the curd thickens. Remove from heat and store in a sterilised screw-top jar. Keeps for 2 weeks if stored in refrigerator.
Makes one cup.

To obtain coconut cream

There is nothing in the world like fresh, rich coconut cream, with its plump, velvety texture and slightly fatty, rich, virginal taste. Especially not the canned stuff.

1 coconut
hot water

Buy a coconut that feels heavy in the hand. Hold the coconut in one hand over a bowl to catch the juices. Crack it open by smacking it, around its circumference, with the back of a heavy Chinese cleaver. Catch the juices in the bowl and save for drinking later. Grate the meat with the sharp prongs of a coconut grater, known as a 'rabbit', or continue cracking the shell of the coconut and loosen the 'meat' away from the pieces of shell. Grate the coconut meat against a strong grater. Add hot water to just cover coconut meat, and leave to soak for 10 minutes or until water is cool. Squeeze the juice from the meat into another bowl through a fine-meshed sieve or dampened muslin and stand for 30 minutes to allow the cream to rise to the top. Use the same day, in curries, sea-food sauces, or drizzled over fresh mango or other tropical fruit. P.S. Add more hot water to just cover the squeezed meat, then squeeze and leave for 30 minutes to make a thinner milk.

To pickle vegetables

Pickle your own Chinese vegetables (*dai ga jeung*) and you'll have a regular supply to have with rice, or to serve as an appetiser before a Chinese meal. Use dry, clean chopsticks when removing pickled vegetables from the jar, to avoid contaminating the brine.

1 white radish (lo bak)
2 carrots
10 radishes
1 onion
1 large piece ginger, peeled
1 cup cauliflower florets
2 small red chillies
2 tbsp salt
2 tbsp rice wine vinegar
2 litres (3½ pints) water

Peel white radish and carrots and cut into slices, and then into strips. Peel onion and radishes and cut into wedges, then cut wedge in half. Peel ginger and cut into thin slices. Wash all vegetables and dry thoroughly. Bring water to the boil and add ginger slices, chillies, salt and rice wine vinegar. Remove from heat and allow to cool. Layer vegetables in a large sterilised jar, then top with the brine. Cover with greaseproof paper and tie securely with string. Set aside in a cool place for 3 days before using.
Feeds four.

To roast a chicken

This is the finest, and simplest way to roast a whole bird. It's borrowed from the French, but don't let that stop you serving it with Mum's gravy (Broths and Sauces, 208) or bread sauce (Broths and Sauces, 206) and plenty of fresh green peas.

1.5 or 1.6 kg chicken (3 to 4 lb)
1 lemon
sea salt
freshly ground black pepper

Heat oven to 200°C (400°F).
Wash chicken in cold water and pat dry. Reach into the cavity and pull off any fat that remains inside the entrance. Squeeze lemon juice over and inside the chicken, rubbing it into the skin. Rub chicken inside and out with sea salt and pepper, and pop the squeezed lemon into the cavity. Melt the chicken fat in a small frypan while you truss the chicken with string, tying the legs and wings firmly in place. Place chicken on a wire rack inside the roasting pan. Fill pan with hot water until it almost reaches the level of the rack. Pour most of the melted chicken fat over the chicken, and roast for 30 minutes. Turn chicken around in oven, baste with remaining chicken fat and roast for a further 30 minutes at 180°C (350°F) or until the skin is golden and the leg moves easily when jiggled. If you're not sure, pierce the area between leg and breast with the tip of a knife. If the juices run clear, the chicken is cooked. Leave chicken in a warm place for 10 minutes before carving.
Feeds four.

To roast red peppers

The world went mad about roast peppers a few years ago, and very nearly took all the fun out of them. They should be roasted and dressed on the day of eating, when they are intense and rewarding. For a faster result, grill peppers until the skin blisters, instead of roasting. Serve simply dressed with extra virgin olive oil, sea salt and pepper, or add an anchovy and some capers to the dressing for extra bite.

4 red peppers (capsicums)
1 tbsp olive oil
2 tbsp extra virgin olive oil

Heat oven to 200°C (400°F).
Rub peppers with olive oil and bake for 20 to 30 minutes until the skin bubbles and darkens. Place in a covered bowl for 10 minutes. Peel off and discard the skin. Cut in half, discard seeds, and cut the flesh into long strips, as you require it. Drizzle with extra virgin olive oil and cover until required.
Feeds four.

To pickle beetroot

Lightly pickled beetroot is a great Australian favourite, making its way into salads, hamburgers, and sandwiches. I love serving it finely diced and just warmed through as a vegetable with roast meats and game dishes.

500 ml (18 fl oz) good vinegar
10 cloves
1 level tbsp salt
2 level tbsp sugar
10 peppercorns
6 cooked and peeled beetroot

Mix vinegar, cloves, salt, sugar, and peppercorns in a saucepan and bring to the boil. Simmer for 5 minutes. Cool, and strain. Slice beetroot and stack in an airtight jar. Cover with cooled liquid and seal. Store in refrigerator.
Feeds four.

To frost grapes

This is one of those silly, useless things to do, but frosted grapes look pretty, and taste as they look. Serve at the end of a summer meal with a great glass of muscat, or use as an edible decoration for cake.

6 small, perfect bunches of grapes
1 egg white
1 cup sugar

Wash grapes, and dry carefully. Whisk egg white lightly. Use a basting brush to brush egg white onto the grapes, covering only the areas that will come in contact with the sugar. Dip or roll grapes lightly in caster sugar, then lay on a flat plate. Chill in refrigerator for several hours.
Feeds six.

To cut green onion flowers

In China, the carving of delicate fruits and vegetables has been an art form since the Tang dynasty (AD 618–906). Making our green (spring) onions more attractive is the least we can do to uphold tradition.

1 bunch green (spring) onions

Trim roots from green onions. Cut white part of stems into 5 cm (2 in) lengths and green part of stems into 3 cm (1½ in) lengths. Use the tip of a sharp knife to cut each end of a white piece of stem into very fine strips, to one-third the length of the piece. Cut only one end of a green piece of stem along its length into very fine strips, to halfway only. Place both green and white lengths in a bowl of cold water chilled with ice blocks. Leave bowl in refrigerator for 1 hour, where the cut lengths will curl apart into flower shapes. Leave in cold water until ready to serve.

Bibliography

Beard, James. *James Beard's American Cookery*. Little, Brown and Company, Boston, 1972.

Bond, Jules M. *The – Cuisine I Love* (Italian, Hungarian, Jewish, Spanish, Viennese). Leon Amiel, New York, 1977.

Boni, Ada. *Italian Regional Cooking*. Godfrey Cave Associates, London, 1982.

Campbell, Dolly. *I Hate To Cook*. Mandarin, Melbourne, 1991.

Castelvetro, Giacomo. *The Fruit, Herbs & Vegetables of Italy*. Viking, London, 1989.

Cipriani, Arrigo. *The Harry's Bar Cookbook*. Smith Gryphon, London, 1991.

David, Elizabeth. *French Provincial Cooking*. Penguin, Harmondsworth, 1970.

De' Medici, Lorenza. *The Heritage of Italian Cooking*. Weldon Russell Publishing, Australia, 1990.

Del Conte, Anna. *Gastronomy of Italy*. Transworld Publishers, London, 1987.

Di Stasio, Rinaldo, Durack, Terry, and Dupleix, Jill. *Allegro Al Dente*. William Heinemann Australia, 1994.

Dominé, Andre, and Ditter, Michael (chief editors). *Culinaria*, volumes 1 and 2. Konemann, Cologne, 1995.

Domingo, Xavier. *The Taste of Spain*. Flammarion, Paris, 1992.

Drake, Miss. *Every Lady's Cook-book*. Swinburne Technical College, Victoria, year unknown.

Edwards, John. *The Roman Cookery of Apicius*. Century, London, 1984.

Fussell, Betty. *I Hear America Cooking*. Viking, New York, 1986.

Ghedini, Francesco. *Northern Italian Cooking*. Gramercy Publishing Company, New York, 1979.

Gozzini Giacosa, Ilaria. *A Taste of Ancient Rome*. University of Chicago Press, 1992.

Grigson, Jane. *Charcuterie and French Pork Cookery*. Penguin Books, Harmondsworth, 1970.

Hayes, Babette. *200 Years of Australian Cooking*. Thomas Nelson, London, 1970.

Hazan, Marcella. *The Classic Italian Cookbook*. Macmillan, London, 1973.

Lang, George. *The Cuisine of Hungary*. Atheneum, New York, 1982.

Larousse Gastronomique, Paul Hamlyn, London, 1994.

Leeming, Margaret and Huang Man-hui, May. *Chinese Regional Cookery*. Rider, London, 1983.

Lin, Hsiang Ju and Lin, Tsuifeng. *Chinese Gastronomy*. Thomas Nelson, London, 1969.

Little, Alastair. *Alastair Little's Italian Kitchen*. Ebury Press, London, 1996.

Mariani, John. *The Dictionary of American Food and Drink*. Hearst Books, New York, 1994.

Milne, A.A. *Pooh's Little Instruction Book*. Methuen, London, 1995.

P.W.M.U. Cookery Book. Lothian Publishing, Melbourne, 1973.

Patten, Marguerite. *Classic British Dishes*. Bloomsbury, London, 1994.

Pépin, Jacques. *La Technique*. Papermac, London, 1982,

Rhodes, Gary. *Rhodes Around Britain*. BBC Books, London, 1994.

Roden, Claudia. *A New Book of Middle Eastern Food*. Penguin Cookery Library, Harmondsworth, 1985.

Rosengarten, David. *The Dean & Deluca Cookbook*. Random House, New York, 1996.

Santolini, Antonella. *Roma in bocca*. Edikronos, Palermo, 1980.

Sevilla, Maria Jose. *Spain on a Plate*. BBC Books, London, 1992.

So, Yan-kit. *Classic Food of China*. Macmillan, London, 1992.

Stewart, Katie. *Cooking & Eating*. Hart-Davis, Macgibbon, London, 1975.

The Mothers Book Committee, Bialik College Parents Association. *I Love To Eat Jewish*. Port Phillip Press, Melbourne, 1980.

Time Life. *The Foods of the World* series. Time Life Books, New York.

Tower, Jeremiah. *New American Classics*. Harper & Row, New York, 1986.

Tsuji, Shizuo. *Japanese Cooking: a Simple Art*. Kodansha, Tokyo, 1981.

Willan, Anne. *French Regional Cooking*. Hutchinson, London, 1981.

Willson, Carol, Goode, John, and Kaydos, Liz. *Greek-Australian Cookbook*. Kangaroo Press, Sydney, 1982.

Wong, Ella-mei. *The Genuine Chinese Cook Book*. Child & Henry, Sydney, 1983.

arborio rice Tough, plump superfino rice grown in Northern Italy. Brilliant for risotto and rice pudding.

belacan, also **blachan** Dried shrimp paste from Malaysia that smells vile until it is cooked.

bocconcini Small fresh balls of snowy white mozzarella cheese, stored in their own whey.
Used in salads, antipasti and pizze. The best are made from buffalo milk.

bonito flakes Dried shavings of bonito, a fish of the mackerel family, used in making dashi stock and for flavouring Japanese soups.

bread By bread I generally mean good, tough, country-style sourdough. Seek out a baker with a wood-fired oven and a commitment to organically grown flour and natural leavening.

bruschetta Usually refers to a slice of grilled, garlicky bread, drizzled with extra virgin olive oil. I have taken liberties with tradition, with both strawberry (Breakfast, 6) and goats cheese (Supper, 192) versions.

bulghur, also **burghul** Cracked wheat.

cabbage, Chinese My favourites are the flowering cabbage (choy sum), with pale green stems and small yellow flowers; the long, pale Peking or Tsientsin cabbage (wong nga bak) with leaves similar to a Savoy; Chinese broccoli (gai laan); and baby (Shanghai) bok choy cabbages, crisp stems with leafy tops and tender hearts.

campari A bitter red apéritif created by Gaspare Campari for his Caffe Campari, which opened in Milan in 1867. My considerable research seems to suggest a glass of Campari and soda with a twist of orange before dinner makes you a better cook.

candlenuts A round beige nut used to thicken and add a sweet nutty flavour to Thai and Malaysian dishes.
Substitute macadamia nuts.

cha plu leaves Small, edible, glossy, pointed green leaves (Piper sarmentosum) related to betel leaves, and used in Thai, Laotian and Vietnamese cooking.

chile, ancho A sweet, fruity, dried poblano, a fresh green Mexican chile.

chile, fresh serrano Green or red cylindrical chile with a tapered end and good, clean heat.

chile, pasilla Long, dark, dried chile also known as chile negro.

chilli bean sauce A Sichuan (Northern Chinese) paste of soy beans and chilli that packs quite a punch.

chilli sambal, sambal oelek Cooked red chilli paste with soy sauce, from Indonesia.

Chinese mushrooms (shiitake) Available fresh or dried. Soak dried mushrooms in warm water for 20 minutes, squeeze gently and discard stems. Use the soaking water as a mushroom broth for cooking.

Chinese rice wine Yellow rice wine made from glutinous rice.

chorizo A Spanish pork sausage flavoured with paprika and garlic, sold dried or fresh.

cornflour, also **cornstarch** Avoid overuse, but it is handy for thickening sauces at the last minute.

cous cous Tiny pearls of semolina which, when steamed, become a dish (also) known as cous cous throughout the Middle East.

couverture, chocolate The finest chocolate you can use, with the highest percentage of cocoa butter (look for 60% to 70%) and very little sugar.

cream Look for the percentage of milk fat on the label to determine the type of cream. Thick cream of 45% milk fat is also known as double cream (UK) and heavy cream (US). Cream of 35% milk fat is also known as single cream (UK) and light cream (US).

curry leaves Sold fresh or dried in Asian and Indian stores.

daikon radish Giant, white, Japanese radish with a mild, refreshing flavour.

dashi The essential Japanese broth, made of konbu (kelp) and dried bonito (fish). Make your own (Broths and Sauces, 206), or mix 10 g (½ oz) of instant dashi powder with 500 ml (18 fl oz) hot water.

dried red chillies Long, red, dried chillies that need soaking, squeezing dry and pounding into a paste before use in Malaysian cooking.

dried shrimps Tiny little pink sundried shrimps. Soak in water before use.

duck or **goose fat** Available in cans for those not up to rendering their own. Store in refrigerator and use sparingly but memorably for cooking potatoes and onions, basting roast chicken, and for slow-cooking duck in the confit style.

fish sauce, Thai A thin, salty sauce made from fermented fish and squid, used as a condiment and cooking sauce.
Known as nuoc mam in Vietnam and nam pla in Thailand.

galangal A ginger-like plant also known as laos and Siamese ginger, used in Thai cooking.

golden syrup A light golden treacle used in sweets and puddings. Substitute corn syrup.

Japanese pickled ginger Sushi's best friend, beni shoga, pickled slices of ginger made by salting fresh ginger and marinating it in rice vinegar and sugar.

jellyfish, dried Popular in China and Japan as a textural, sea-tasting treat, in spite of looking like chamois. Soak for a few hours, in several changes of water and blanch in boiling water before cutting into fine ribbons and tossing in a salad.

juniper berries Small dark berries used to flavour gin. Particularly nice with pork, game, rabbit and kangaroo dishes.

kaiserfleisch Austrian smoked and cured pork, available in the piece.

kasseler The smoked eye of the loin of pork, usually sold cooked and sold by the rib or slice.

konbu Giant sea kelp, harvested off the shores of Hokkaido. Along with bonito, it forms the basis of Japanese dashi stock. Sold dried in cellophane packs.

lemon grass A perfumed stalk that requires peeling before finely chopping the white base. Or bash the stalks and infuse in boiling water to make a delicate tea.

mascarpone A fresh thick, gooey, gorgeous cream cheese made of cow's milk, the inspiration for tira misu and other irresistible Italian desserts.

mirin Sweet rice wine with low alcohol content, used in Japanese cooking.

miso A fermented paste made from soya beans

morcilla sausages Strong, smoky, spicy Spanish sausages made of pig's blood.

noodles, rice stick Sticks of dry, flat, white, semi-transparent rice flour noodles popular in Vietnam and Thailand.

noodles, soba Light brown Japanese buckwheat noodles, served cold with dipping sauce or in hot soups.

nori Dark green dried sheets of seaweed, used to wrap rice in rolls, and to garnish savoury dishes.

palm sugar Sweet brown caramel-tasting sugar made from the sap of the palmyra palm, used in Thailand and Malaysia.

piquillo peppers Fleshy, sweet, red, hot, Spanish peppers, often roasted in wood-fired ovens.

red shallots Eschalots, small brown- to red-skinned onions with a milder flavour than large onions.

rose water syrup A clear, fragrant syrup extracted from rose petals, available from Middle Eastern stores. Use only a drop or two if you can only find the much stronger rose water essence.

saffron Buy the red-golden threads, strands of the dried stigma of the crocus flower, and crush them in a mortar with a tiny amount of water or broth before adding to your cooking. (Try saffron mash, it's fabulous.)

sago, pearl Small pearls made of starchy stuff extracted from certain palm trees. When cooked, they turn transparent.

sake Fermented rice wine from Japan.

salted radish Known as hua pak gart kao in Thailand, and often labelled 'salted turnip'.

shallots, deep-fried Deep-fried thin slices of small red shallots, sold in airtight tubs in Asian food stores.

Sichuan peppercorns The seed from the peppery ash tree (fagara), with a peppery, prickly flavour.

Sichuan preserved vegetable Mustard green roots preserved in salt and chilli, usually sold in cans.

soy sauce, dark Aged soy that, while heavier than light soy, actually tastes less salty.

soy sauce, light A thin soy that is fresh and salty.

speck In Europe, speck is pork fat. In Australia, it is often confused with kaiserfleisch or other smoked pork products.

star anise Fragrant star-shaped spice with a licorice-like flavour, native to China.

tamarind Sour-tasting tamarind is extracted from the pods of tamarind trees and compressed into blocks of pulpy stuff. Available from Asian and Latin American food stores.

tofu, fresh Cakes of freshly pressed beancurd, stored in water, and sold in packets of six. Use quickly, and change water daily.

tofu, hard A firm beancurd, made from soy beans and sold in vacuum packs in Oriental food stores.

tomato passato A sauce made purely of fresh tomatoes, passed through a sieve.

tomato paste A concentrated tomato purée sold in tubes, jars and tins.

tortilla Flat unleavened pancakes made with either corn or wheat flour and cooked on a griddle.

wakame Dried sea kelp which expands dramatically when soaked in water. Used to flavour soups.

wasabi A green pungent root known as Japanese horseradish, it is grated to form a paste that has the kick of a mule. You can buy it ready-made in tubes, or as a powder.

won ton wrappers Thin square sheets of dough made from eggs and wheat flour, terrific for dumplings and ravioli. Available from Asian food stores.

wood ear fungus, or **cloud ear fungus** A black fungus that grows naturally on rotting wood, sold dried. Soak well, and trim stems before use.

P.S. Good food is universal, but specific labelling is not. Prawns (Aust. and UK) are shrimp (US), minced beef (Aust. and UK) is ground beef (US), plain flour (Aust. and UK) is all-purpose flour (US), caster sugar (Aust. and UK) is superfine sugar (US), icing sugar (Aust. and UK) is confectioner's sugar (US), tomato paste (Aust. and US) is tomato purée (UK), sultanas (Aust. and UK) are seedless white raisins (US), eggplants (Aust. and US) are aubergines (UK), and green or red peppers (Aust.) are capsicums (UK) and bell peppers (US).

Gratitude

To my grandmother, Doris May Campbell.
To my mother, father, sisters, brother, niece, nephew and sister-in-law, for keeping me honest.
To Sue Hines, first for *New Food* and now for this.
To Visnja Brdar, for truth and beauty in a book.

To Arunas, for the author photograph on the jacket; to Sally-Ann Balharrie for the photograph on page 21; to Anna Bertalli, for the photographs on pages 7, 15; to Visnja Brdar, for the photograph on page v; to Earl Carter, for the photograph on page 37; to Mark Chew, for the photographs on pages 5, 55, 215; to Simon Griffiths, for the photograph on page 222; to Geoff Lung, for the photographs on pages 127, 157; to Ashley Mackevicius, for the photographs on pages 9, 11, 13, 23, 29, 31, 51, 57, 59, 63, 65, 69, 71, 75, 91, 119, 129, 131, 137, 139, 151, 133, 189, 193, 199, 200; and to Petrina Tinslay, for the photographs on pages 17, 25, 27, 33, 39, 41, 43, 47, 49, 73, 79, 81, 82, 87, 89, 93, 97, 101, 103, 105, 109, 111, 115, 117, 121, 123, 135, 140, 145, 147, 149, 153, 159, 161, 163, 165, 167, 169, 173, 175, 177, 179, 181, 183, 185, 191, 197, 205, 211.

To Barry McDonald, for the peaches; Sibella Court, for the cute props; Phillip Holmes, for the cocktails; The Monarch, for the German plum cake; Margie Agostini, for the brownies; Dietmar Sawyere, for the artichoke; Annabel Savill, for the grilled seafood; Daryll Taylor, for the croque-monsieur; Luke Mangan, for the snow eggs; Maurizio Terzini, for the bicicletta; Jeremiah Tower, for the cole slaw; George Lang, for the gulyas; Paul Bocuse, for the rabbit rillettes; Maria Battaglia, for the broken pasta; Mum, for the gravy; the woman who rang me while I was on the radio, for help with my roesti; Appley Hoare Antiques, Orson & Blake and The Bay Tree, for heaps of stuff; and Gaspare Campari and Jacob Schweppes, for keeping me going.

And to Terry Durack, for everything else.

First published in 1998. A Sue Hines Book. Allen & Unwin Pty Ltd
9 Atchison Street, St Leonards, NSW 2065 Australia. Phone: 61 2 9901 4088 Fax: 61 2 9906 2218
E-mail: frontdesk@allen-unwin.com.au. URL: http://www.allen-unwin.com.au

National Library of Australia. Cataloguing-in-Publication entry:
Dupleix, Jill.
Old food: new ways with old favourites.
Includes index and bibliography.
ISBN 1 86448 348 2.
1. Cookery. I. Title
641.5

10 9 8 7 6 5 4 3 2 1

Designed by Visnja Brdar, Brdar Design.
Typeset by J & M Typesetting.
Printed by South China Printing Co.